Mastering Unity

Mastering Computer Science

Series Editor: Sufyan bin Uzayr

Mastering Unity: A Beginner's Guide
Divya Sachdeva and Aruqqa Khateib

Mastering Unreal Engine: A Beginner's Guide
Divya Sachdeva and Aruqqa Khateib

Mastering UI Mockups and Frameworks: A Beginner's Guide
Mohamed Musthafa MC and Kapil Kishnani

Mastering Ruby on Rails: A Beginner's Guide
Mathew Rooney and Madina Karybzhanova

Mastering Sketch: A Beginner's Guide
Mathew Rooney and Md Javed Khan

Mastering Java: A Beginner's Guide
Divya Sachdeva and Natalya Ustukpayeva

For more information about this series, please visit: https://www.routledge.com/Mastering-Computer-Science/book-series/MCS

The "Mastering Computer Science" series of books are authored by the Zeba Academy team members, led by Sufyan bin Uzayr.

Zeba Academy is an EdTech venture that develops courses and content for learners primarily in STEM fields, and offers education consulting to Universities and Institutions worldwide. For more info, please visit https://zeba.academy

Mastering Unity

A Beginner's Guide

Edited by Sufyan bin Uzayr

CRC Press
Taylor & Francis Group
Boca Raton London New York

CRC Press is an imprint of the
Taylor & Francis Group, an **informa** business

First edition published 2022
by CRC Press

6000 Broken Sound Parkway NW, Suite 300, Boca Raton, FL 33487-2742

and by CRC Press
2 Park Square, Milton Park, Abingdon, Oxon, OX14 4RN

CRC Press is an imprint of Taylor & Francis Group, LLC

ISBN: 9781032103198 (hbk)
ISBN: 9781032103174 (pbk)
ISBN: 9781003214755 (ebk)

DOI: 10.1201/9781003214755

Typeset in Minion
by KnowledgeWorks Global Ltd.

Contents

About the Editor

Sufyan bin Uzayr is a writer, coder, and entrepreneur with more than a decade of experience in the industry. He has authored several books in the past, pertaining to a diverse range of topics, ranging from History to Computers/IT.

Sufyan is the Director of Parakozm, a multinational IT company specializing in EdTech solutions. He also runs Zeba Academy, an online learning and teaching vertical with a focus on STEM fields.

Sufyan specializes in a wide variety of technologies, such as JavaScript, Dart, WordPress, Drupal, Linux, and Python. He holds multiple degrees, including ones in Management, IT, Literature, and Political Science.

Sufyan is a digital nomad, dividing his time between four countries. He has lived and taught in universities and educational institutions around the globe. Sufyan takes a keen interest in technology, politics, literature, history, and sports, and in his spare time, he enjoys teaching coding and English to young students.

Learn more at sufyanism.com.

CHAPTER 1

Introduction to Unity

Unity is a sophisticated cross-platform integrated development environment (IDE) for developers as well as a three- and two-dimensional (3D/2D) game engine. Let's take a closer look at what this entails.

Like a game engine, Unity can provide many of the most crucial built-in elements that make a game run. This includes physics, 3D rendering, and collision detection. From the standpoint of a developer, this indicates that there is no need to reinvent the wheel. Instead of starting a new project by developing a new physics engine from the ground up—calculating every individual movement of each substance or the way light should bounce off various surfaces.

What makes Unity even more potent is the presence of a booming "Asset Store." This is simply a location where

DOI: 10.1201/9781003214755-1

developers may post their inventions and share them with the community.

Want a stunning fire effect and do not have the time to create one from scratch? We should be able to find something in the asset store. Want to add tilt controls to our game without the time-consuming process of fine-tuning the sensitivity? There is most likely an asset for that as well.

All of this means that the game developer can concentrate on what is important: creating a unique and enjoyable experience while coding just the elements specific to that vision.

WHAT EXACTLY IS THE UNITY IDE?

Unity is an IDE as well as a game engine. The term "integrated development environment" refers to an interface that provides access to all development tools in one location. The Unity program has a visual editor that allows developers to drag and drop items into scenes and adjust their characteristics.

The Unity Software also includes a slew of other essential features and tools, such as browsing between project folders and creating animations using a timeline tool.

When it comes to coding, Unity will use an alternate editor of your choosing. The most prevalent option is Microsoft's Visual Studio, which integrates most of the time.

What Is the Language Used by Unity?

Unreal utilizes C# to manage code and logic, with a slew of classes and application programming interface (APIs) that you'll need to understand. The good news is that you can do a lot in Unity without dealing with a lot of code. However, knowing how to program opens up many new possibilities for what you can do, and Unity allows you to customize practically anything.

Fortunately, C# is also one of the more approachable programming languages for beginners. It's also well worth knowing because it's extensively used in the business and has a lot in common with other prominent languages like C and Java. In other words, studying Unity with C# is a terrific way to get started with coding.

What Is Unity 3D, and How Is It Used?

Simply said, Unity is the most popular gaming engine in the world. It has many features and is versatile enough to create practically any game you can think of.

Unity is popular among both amateur developers and AAA studios because of its unequaled cross-platform functionality. It's been used to make games such as Pokemon GO, Hearthstone, RimWorld, Cuphead, and many more.

While the name implies 3D, Unity 3D also includes capabilities for 2D game production.

Because of the C# scripting API and built-in Visual Studio integration, programmers adore it. For those looking for an alternative to Visual Studio, Unity provides JavaScript as a scripting language and MonoDevelop as an IDE.

On the other hand, designers adore it since it has robust animation tools that make it simple to create our 3D sequences or develop 2D animations from scratch. In Unity, almost anything can be animated.

Also, Unity 3D has a free version that allows creators to release games produced using Unity Personal without paying for the program as long as they generate less than $100,000 from the games.

For those willing to pay, Unity provides specific additional capabilities and a customizable licensing plan via a tiered subscription approach. Premium customers will also get access to the Unity source code and development assistance.

Because Unity has been around since 2005, it has amassed a significant user base and an incredible library of materials. Not only does Unity offer excellent documentation, but videos and tutorials are abundantly available online.

For this reason alone, beginners should begin using Unity. Unity acts as a knowledge and resource center among many video game engines based simply on its great community.

Other Game Engines vs. Unity

Other large game engines are available for development. Unreal Engine and Cryengine are among the gaming engines that compete with Unity. So, what makes Unity so appealing?

Because you're on an Android website, you're probably interested in mobile development. This is where Unity shines as a programming tool. While it was once known as "Unity 3D," the program has evolved to be as powerful as a 2D creation tool. Not only has that, but the way visuals are handled made porting experiences to lower-end hardware quite simple.

Unity·powers the great majority of products on the Google Play Store for these reasons.

However, because Unity is cross-platform, making games on iOS, PC, or even gaming consoles is just as simple. Unity also provides outstanding virtual reality (VR) compatibility for developers who want to create apps for the Oculus Rift or HTC Vive.

Unity 3D Game Development

Graphics, networks, technological augmentation, and real-time performance have all evolved tremendously in game development. Multiple market participants currently seek to provide game creation and development to more people and across more platforms.

One game engine stands out from the crowd: Unity 3D. It is a sophisticated game engine that works on several platforms and is highly user-friendly for both professionals and beginners. Unity 3D is the game engine to choose if you want a sophisticated game engine that can generate real-world images without consuming much computing power.

Consider these statistics! Unity is responsible for 34% of the free mobile games available on the Google Play Store and the Apple App Store. Isn't it fascinating? Unity 3D's gaming platforms have assisted in developing games that have reached more than 500 million players globally, a figure that is growing year after year. Without question, it is one of the most popular gaming engines on the market.

Unity 3D Gaming Solutions: Unity 3D gaming solutions are among the finest in the industry. The cross-platform engine aids game creators in creating games that may be utilized in a variety of contexts, including:

- **PC and Console Games:** This provides rich graphics and developer-friendly tools and toolkits, which not only boosts your capacity to make modifications but also ensures that your games function optimally.
- **Instant Games:** Project Tiny, a flagship product of Unity Technologies, creates light, quick, and compact games with new runtime and stability across segments.
- **Mobile Games:** One of the most popular platforms for using Unity 3D game solutions. This platform is a master in mobile gaming, with device-ready content, optimization, and revenue potential.
- **AR/VR Games:** Augmented/virtual reality (AR/VR) games have grown in popularity over the last decade. Unity 3D makes such ambitions a reality by providing immediate real-time tools that enable a wide range of creative possibilities in AR/VR engines.

In terms of visuals, game creators frequently want their game to be as similar to reality as possible. The images should give the gamer the sensation of "being in the game." Asset shop for Unity3D provides outstanding 3D models for animations, shaders, and textures—components that make the experience more realistic. If we acquire sound effects and gaming assets, Unity 3D allows us to do so since it excels at everything if you want to acquire sound effects.

Consider this: some individuals are brilliant developers, others are great at graphics or animation, and some are fantastic with musical diversity. Unity 3D is a terrific asset tool that helps unite various characteristics into a single platform and create something original and indigenous.

All Gaming Solutions under One Roof

If we seek end-to-end game creation with excellent development modules and additional support and maintenance, Juego Studios is the place to go.

We at Juego Studios offer one of the greatest, if not the most comprehensive, solutions to help you design, create, and promote your product. We are professionals in developing and designing cost-effective, dependable, and expansive game concepts and features.

We are a market leader in game design and game production, providing end-to-end solutions. Our team of over 150 designers, developers, illustrators, animators, graphic designers, and others will assist us in bringing our game from concept to reality.

We create and deliver games for various platforms, including PC, web, mobile, and console. We are gradually developing or leaving our imprint in the creation of AR and VR games. Our various games have garnered multiple honors employing the newest technology and network connectivity. From the 2D platform to the 3D engine to the AR/VR environment, we create games.

Juego Studios takes pleasure in making exciting games that push the boundaries of the industry using the most powerful technologies and frameworks available. We deal with a variety of game engines, but the one showcased here is Unity 3D.

NINE SIGNIFICANT BENEFITS OF UNITY 3D GAME DEVELOPMENT

- **Multiple Platforms:** One of the most important reasons Unity 3D is valued by game creators worldwide is the ability to construct, manage, and deliver cross-platform games. This implies that game creators are not restricted to a single platform and may thus render to over 25 big platforms including mobile, PC, console, television, and, more recently, AR and VR; this type of easiness and flexibility is what makes game creation such an exciting and refreshing vocation.
- **Effective and Reliable:** According to a 2018 research, Unity Technologies and its flagship gaming engine Unity 3D held more than 60% of the market share in the AR and VR field, with more than 40% of mobile gaming platforms using the platform to produce games. It is efficient, dependable, and widely used by players all around the world.
- **Editor and Developer:** Play Mode, Timeline Story Tools, Real-Time Global Illumination, and Comprehensive Memory Profiling with Retargetable Animators are just a few of the features that make Unity 3D a powerful and advanced yet easy-to-use editor.
- **Multiple Rendering:** Unity 3D, which has received several honors for its game creation system, is perhaps one of the top three systems in the world for game rendering and deployment. While it is extremely

quick with 2D rendering models, it is equally excellent with 3D rendering.

- **Play Mode:** One of the most excellent tools for quick iterative editing is Play Mode. The play mode function in Unity 3D is one of the game engine's most popular features. It allows the developer to quickly see and play inside the game and test and evaluate it. It facilitates the convenience of testing how things can work out without much difficulty. If one meets a glitch or believes the game isn't running correctly, it can be paused and tweaked to the game developer's satisfaction, promptly updating results. Frame-to-frame referencing is also possible in Play or Play Plus Mode.

- **Multiplayer Systems:** Using the Unity 3D platform is one of the most straightforward ways to develop a networked and real-time gaming system. This game engine's outstanding multiplayer experience is not only flexible but also quickly implemented and expandable. Unity 3D allows you to create integrated multiplayer systems that leverage matchmakers and relay servers as a platform.

- **Great Visual Experience:** Unity 3D is a fantastic visual platform and an excellent platform for developing visual experience games. The application is fantastic, and it is less complicated and easy when compared to many other technologies.

- **Analytics:** Unity 3D has analytics that any game developer or client may access through the editor.

With Unity Analytics, we can get, discover, and use game-related insights. It may provide you with valuable information to establish a more robust platform and make tiny tweaks to offer a fantastic experience for the gamers.

- **Developer Community:** The Unity Developer Community is a forum for all developers to come and discuss their issues and recommendations for enhancing the system and get immediate familiarity with the engine.

Overall, Unity 3D Game Development is a multi-platform, all-in-one product. Game creators may import games created on other platforms such as iOS, PC, Play Store, and game consoles. Developers can opt to make just minor changes to their games to take full use of Unity 3D's features.

Options for Licensing

Unity has three pricing tiers: personal, plus, and professional.

While the free version will get you started, we'll want to upgrade to plus or pro if we're serious about producing commercial games.

Those who do not pay the monthly subscription must prove earnings of less than $100,000 for the games they create with Unity.

Hobbyists may subscribe to the Plus plan to obtain access to additional features and training materials, which will help them monetize their games and enhance their skills. This is wonderful for indie devs that are just getting started with Unity development.

The Pro tier is intended for game studios and professional teams that require in-house assistance and those that earn more than $200,000 from Unity projects.

Overall Views

We've been using Unity 3D for many years so that we can share firsthand comments and pitfalls.

First and foremost, we believe Unity is an excellent engine. It's not the finest, but it's a fantastic, well-rounded tool that's ideal for novices.

Second, there is no such thing as the most refined gaming engine. There are only tools available for the job. Some are superior to others, and it all depends on the requirements of the unique project. While we'll need coding abilities to utilize Unity, tools can help us learn anything we choose.

A short Google search yields code samples and materials for everything from first-person shooters to candy-crush-style matching games and everything in between. However, there are compelling reasons to master coding in addition to 3D/computer graphics (CG) jobs. Unity is, at its core, a well-rounded game engine that simplifies game production. While there may be better engines to use based on our project's requirements, understanding Unity can only help us improve as a game developer.

Unity is the way to go if we're a complete newbie because the community will assist learns, and the tools will last a long time. If we're more experienced, we could prefer

Unity due to its cross-platform deployment possibilities and quicker development process. Keep in mind that many AAA game developers use Unity, making it a solid choice in the vast field of video games.

System Requirements for Unity Editor

- **System Requirements**
    - **Operating system version:** Windows 7 (SP1+), Windows 10, and Windows 11, 64-bit versions only.
    - **CPU:** X64 architecture with SSE2 instruction set support.
    - **Graphics API:** DX10, DX11, and DX12-capable GPUs.
    - **Additional requirements:** Hardware vendor officially supported drivers.

System Requirements for Unity Player

- **Mobile**
    - **Operating system**
    - **Version:** 4.4 (API 19)+
    - **CPU:** ARMv7 with Neon Support (32-bit) or ARM64
    - **Graphics API:** OpenGL ES 2.0+, OpenGL ES 3.0+, and Vulkan
    - **Additional requirements:** 1GB+ RAM

- **Desktop**
    - **Operating system**
    - **Version:** Windows 7 (SP1+), Windows 10, and Windows 11.
    - **CPU:** x86, x64 architecture with SSE2 instruction set support.
    - **Graphics API:** DX10, DX11, DX12 capable.
    - **Additional requirements:** Drivers were officially supported by the hardware vendor.

The Intermediate Language To C++ (IL2CPP) scripting backend requires Visual Studio 2015 with the C++ Tools component or later and the Windows 10 SDK for development.

ARCHITECTURE OF UNITY

The Unity engine is written in native C/C++, but we interface with it through a C# layer. As a result, we must be familiar with some of the fundamental notions of C# scripting. This part of the User Manual describes how Unity implements .NET and C#, as well as any errors you may see when coding.

.NET Overview in Unity

Unity takes advantage of the open-source .NET platform to ensure that apps created with Unity may operate on a broad range of hardware configurations. .NET provides support for various languages and API libraries.

Backend Scripting

Unity features two scripting backends: Mono and IL2CPP (Intermediate Language To C++), each with its compilation technique:

- Mono employs just-in-time (JIT) compilation and builds code as needed during runtime.
- IL2CPP employs ahead-of-time (AOT) compilation, which builds our complete program before execution.

The advantage of employing a JIT-based scripting backend is that it compiles significantly quicker than AOT and is platform-independent.

The Unity Editor is JIT-based, with Mono serving as the scripting backend. We may select which programming backend to utilize when creating a player for your application. To accomplish this in the Editor, go to Edit > Project Settings > Player, open the Other Settings panel, click on the Scripting Backend option and pick the desired backend.

Directed Code Stripping

When you develop your program, Unity searches the built assemblies (.DLLs) for unnecessary code and removes it. This method minimizes the final binary size of our build while increasing build time.

When using Mono, code stripping is disabled by default; however, code stripping cannot be deactivated for IL2CPP. Unity's aggressiveness while stripping code may be adjusted. Open the Other Settings panel, click the Managed Stripping Level dropdown, and pick the code level denying that desire.

Collection of Garbage

For both the Mono and IL2CPP backend, Unity employs the Boehm garbage collector. By default, Unity employs the Incremental mode. Although Unity suggests using Incremental mode, you may disable it to employ "stop the world" trash collection.

To switch between Incremental mode and "stop the world," navigate Edit > Project Settings > Player, open the Other Settings panel, and tick the Use incremental GC checkbox. In Incremental mode, Unity's garbage collector runs for a limited duration and may not always gather all objects in a single pass. This distributes the time it takes to acquire things across many frames, reducing stuttering and CPU spikes.

Use the Unity Profiler to examine the amount of allocations and potential CPU spikes in your application. We may also use the GarbageCollector API to deactivate trash collection entirely in players. When the collector is turned off, we should take care not to allocate too much memory.

System Libraries for .NET

Unity supports a wide range of systems and may employ a variety of scripting backend depending on the platform. In several circumstances, the .NET system libraries require platform-specific implementations to function correctly. While Unity makes every effort to support as much of the .NET ecosystem as possible, there are several exceptions to sections of the .NET system libraries that Unity expressly does not support.

Unity offers no assurances about the speed or allocation of the .NET system libraries across Unity versions. Unity, as a general rule, does not correct any performance regressions in the .NET system libraries.

Unity does not support the System. It is not guaranteed that the drawing library will function on all systems.

A JIT scripting backend allows us to generate dynamic C#/.NET Intermediate Language (IL) code during the runtime of our application, whereas an AOT scripting backend does not. This is critical to keep in mind while using third-party libraries since they may utilize distinct code paths for JIT and AOT or employ code paths that rely on dynamically produced code.

Although Unity supports multiple .NET API profiles, for all new applications, we should utilize the .NET Standard 2.0 API Compatibility Level for the following reasons:

- Because .NET Standard 2.0 has a lower API surface, it also has a smaller implementation. The size of our final executable file is reduced as a result of this.
- Because .NET Standard 2.0 has improved cross-platform compatibility, our code is more likely to run on all platforms.
- Because .NET Standard 2.0 is supported by all .NET runtimes, our code will function in a broader range of VM/runtime scenarios (e.g., .NET Framework, .NET Core, Xamarin, Unity).
- More mistakes are moved to the build time in .NET Standard. Several APIs in .NET 4.7.1 are available at build time; however, some platforms' implementations throw an error during runtime.

Other profiles may be handy if we need to support an older existing application, for example. Change the .NET Profile in the Player Settings if we desire a different API compatibility level. To do so, navigate to Edit > Project Settings > Player > Other Settings and choose the desired level from the API Compatibility Level selection.

Making Use of Third-Party .NET Libraries

Third-party .NET libraries should only be used if thoroughly tested on a broad range of Unity setups and systems.

We should profile the use of your .NET system libraries on all target platforms since their performance characteristics may differ based on the scripting backend, .NET versions, and profiles we employ.

Consider the following aspects while reviewing a third-party library:

- **Compatibility:** Some Unity platforms and scripting backend may not be compatible with third-party libraries.
- **Performance:** Third-party libraries may perform significantly differently in Unity than in other .NET runtimes.
- **AOT Binary Size:** Because of the number of dependencies used by the library, third-party libraries may dramatically increase AOT binary size.

Overhead Reflection in C#

All C# reflection (System.Reflection) objects are cached internally by Mono and IL2CPP, and Unity does not trash collect them by design. As a result of this behavior, the garbage collector constantly searches the cached C# reflection objects during the lifetime of our program, causing unnecessary and potentially considerable garbage collector costs.

Avoid approaches such as reducing trash collector overhead Assembly.GetTypes and Type.GetMethods()in our application generates a large number of C# reflection objects at runtime. Instead, scan assemblies in the Editor for the necessary data and serialize and codegen for runtime usage.

UnityEngine.Object Unique Behavior

UnityEngine: In Unity, an object is a specific C# object since it is connected to a native C++ counterpart object. For example, when we utilize a Camera component, Unity does not keep the object's state on the C# object but rather on its native C++ equivalent.

The usage of the C# WeakReference class with UnityEngine.Objects are currently not supported by Unity. As a result, we should never use a WeakReference to refer to a loaded item.

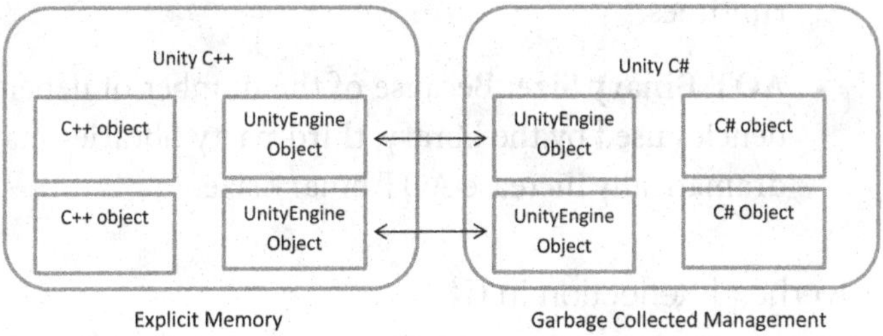

Unity C++
C++ object
UnityEngine Object
C++ object
UnityEngine Object
Explicit Memory
Unity C#
UnityEngine Object
C# object
UnityEngine Object
C# Object
Garbage Collected Management

FIGURE 1.1 Objects in Unity.

UnityEngine Objects Are Shared by Unity C# and Unity C++

When we use a method such as an Object.Destroy or Object.DestroyImmediate to destroy a UnityEngine. Unity removes (unloads) the native counter object when it is derived from an object. Because the garbage collector maintains the memory, we cannot explicitly remove the C# object. The trash collector gathers and destroys the managed object once there are no more references to it.

If a destroyed UnityEngine.Object is reaccessed, Unity recreates the native counterpart object for most types. Two exceptions to this recreation behavior are MonoBehaviour and ScriptableObject:Unity never reloads them once destroyed.

The equality (==) and inequality (!=) operators are overridden by MonoBehaviour and ScriptableObject. When a destroyed MonoBehaviour or ScriptableObject is compared to null, the operators return true if the managed object is still present and has not yet been garbage collected.

Because the ?? and ?. operators are not overloadable, they are incompatible with objects derived from UnityEngine. Object. When used on a destroyed MonoBehaviour or ScriptableObject while the managed object is still active, the operators do not produce the same results as the equality and inequality operators.

Avoid the Use of Async and Await

Because the Unity API is not thread-safe, we should avoid using async and await tasks. When executed, async jobs frequently allocate objects, which might cause performance difficulties if used excessively. Furthermore, Unity does not instantly halt async processes running on managed threads when we quit Play Mode.

In both Edit and Play modes, Unity replaces the default SynchronizationContext with a bespoke UnitySynchronizationContext and executes all tasks on the main thread. To use async tasks, we must manually generate and manage our threads using a TaskFactory, and we must use the default SynchronizationContext rather than the Unity version.

To manually halt the jobs, use EditorApplication.playModeStateChanged to listen for entry and exit play mode events. However, because we are not utilizing the UnitySynchronizationContext, most of the Unity scripting APIs are unavailable.

Reloading Code in the Unity Editor

Domain information reloads and how they affect application performance. It also includes information about running code when the Editor is launched and how to rapidly enter and exit Play mode using Configurable Enter Play Mode.

Serialization of Scripts

Serialization is the act of automatically converting data structures or object states into a format that Unity can store and rebuild later. This section includes information on how to utilize serialization effectively in our Project.

Script Compilation

How and in what sequence Unity builds your programs. This section also includes information on Assembly Definitions and best practices for utilizing them.

WHICH OF THE SEVEN UNITY GAME DEVELOPMENT LANGUAGES SHOULD WE LEARN?

It has never been easier to create games. Unity game development platforms enable the creation of everything from simple 2D platformers to highly sophisticated 3D first-person shooters. Unity is available for free to small developers, and there are several instructions on utilizing the editor to prototype your ideas.

Learning how to utilize the Unity software can only take you so far. The code that dictates the behavior of your game will be the true heart of it. Choosing a language to learn for game production might be difficult, but Unity's case is straightforward.

C# Is the Best Option

C# is the best language to learn for Unity for anyone new to the platform or has prior experience with object-oriented programming. In fact, for a good reason, C# is the only language worth knowing for the platform.

Mono, a cross-platform adaptation of Microsoft's .NET framework, is used by Unity. C# is the core programming language of .NET, and all of Unity's libraries are written in C#. It would not be an exaggeration to state that C# is the language of Unity. Unity has said unequivocally that C# would be the only language supported by the engine in the future.

This is excellent news because C# is a robust language that is also simple to learn. Unity is only one of many compelling reasons to learn C#, and as a novice, we may even find it more approachable. Creating games offers a learning structure, and project-based goals lead to a better comprehension of new subjects.

Unity is pushing the boundaries of what C# can achieve by introducing the C# job system and ECS, and the new Burst compiler makes it quicker than ever before.

JavaScript Is the Current Alternative

UnityScript, which is based on JavaScript, is also supported. Since its first release, JavaScript has coexisted with C# as a fully complete Unity programming language. The Unity scripting documentation included sample code in C# and JavaScript for most of the library's parts.

This was handy for developers from a JavaScript background since they could utilize similar syntax, although variations in the code were organized. There was, however, an issue.

While UnityScript appears to be similar to JavaScript, it is not. UnityScript has classes, whereas JavaScript does not. UnityScript lacks JavaScript features such as multiple variable declaration and optional semi-colons.

Perhaps most importantly, looking for JavaScript expertise on Unity projects has been difficult since most people referred to it as JavaScript rather than UnityScript. The site design and game development results were muddled, and the distinction between the languages was a source of dispute among pure JavaScript developers.

Unsurprisingly, Unity stated that it would discontinue support for UnityScript, and a timeframe for its decommissioning has been established.

The Traditional Third Option: Boo

Boo, a Python-like language, was available in the early days of Unity. This is somewhat unexpected given that Boo's designer, Rodrigo B. De Oliveira, formerly worked with

Unity. The language is .NET and Mono compatible, and it would be completely integrated with the game engine. Where did things go wrong?

Few people used it, most likely because they assumed it was only an attempt to emulate Python. Unity eliminated support for Boo over time, and upcoming UnityScript updates will render all previous Boo scripts obsolete in Unity. Some may consider this a squandered opportunity, as Boo was a fantastic attempt at Python-like syntax for .NET programming.

IronPython Is an Unusual Choice

Python is generally not the language for us if we want to create games, although it is doable. Charlie Calvert explains how to run Python from C# in his Microsoft Developer Community blog, but it's not for the faint of heart. IronPython is still in active development over ten years later.

To summarize, we must get the IronPython libraries from GitHub and include them in your C# project. This allows us to call Python scripts from C# scripts as we would any other library.

IronPython also allows Python to call .NET libraries. As handy as this seems, because Unity is based on C#, it is ineffective.

IronPython and its sister project, IronRuby, which connects C# with the Ruby programming language, are beautiful projects, but they aren't feasible for usage with Unity.

Lua Is an Intriguing Option

MoonSharp—a Lua interpreter—is one of the most acceptable implementations of an external language for Unity.

This project is not intended to replace C# as a programming language but rather serve as a bridge. The ideal use case for MoonSharp would be to provide a means for our game's users to develop game modifications in the Lua programming language.

We might also use it to individually define items and design levels from our primary game code.

MoonSharp is worth considering if we are already working in C# and seeking an exciting method to connect with our code. You may import it straight into our projects because it is accessible on Unity's Asset store.

C/C++ Is the Best Language for Plugins

Despite the rich Unity library and all of the tools provided by C#, we may wish to create our plugins from time to time. The primary reasons people choose plugins are speed and access to a codebase written in another language. Building these scripts into dynamic-link library (DLL) plugins saves time and, in certain circumstances, improves speed.

C++ will be used to create plugins in most situations, although C would work just as well. The code may be stored in Unity's plugin folder and referenced in code as long as it builds into a DLL. However, if we are already familiar with writing in C/C++, learning C# should be a reasonably straightforward effort.

Rust Is a New Programming Language for Plugins

Rust is a language that has a lot of hype about it. Experienced programmers adore it because it provides an enormous degree of control while avoiding the problems of coding in less secure languages such as C++. Mozilla designed rust in 2009 as a tool for developers to construct high-performance applications swiftly.

While it is not feasible to directly write Rust in Unity, we may use Rust-written functions and methods from our Unity code. In his Medium piece, Jim Fleming explains how to accomplish it in detail. If this looks familiar, it's because it's another method for creating Native Plugins. We may use Unity's DllImport feature to access Rust functions straight from C# code by using Rust's ability to interact with other languages. Naturally, there are different stages in between, and reading Jim's follow-up piece and learning about FFIs (foreign function interfaces) is recommended.

- **A Simple Option:** Unity's stance toward any language that isn't C# is unmistakable, and the continuous advancements to Unity rely on this unwavering focus. When we combine this with Microsoft's ongoing enhancements to C# as a language, mastering C# for Unity game production is a no-brainer. Also, for a more straightforward approach to learning game creation, check out Unity Learn.

However, Unity is only one engine among many, and there are several game production software alternatives to select from.

Ten Benefits of the C# Programming Language for Unity Developers

In programming, C# is one of the most accepted, structured, and popular programming languages. C# is widely regarded as one of the most prominent and potent programming languages. One of the compatible languages is C#. It completes work quickly and runs smoothly. In this essay, we will look at the benefits of C# over other programming languages:

- **Object-Oriented Language:** Because C# is an object-oriented language, you may construct modular, maintainable programs and reusable code. This is one of the most significant benefits of C# versus C++.
- **Automatic Rubbish Collection:** C# offers a highly effective technique for erasing and removing all garbage from the system. C# does not cause a mess in the system and does not cause the system to hang during execution.
- **There Is No Problem if Memory Leaks:** C# offers a significant edge in memory backup. Memory leaks and other similar issues would not exist in C#, as they do in C++. In this scenario, C# outperforms all other languages.
- **Easy-to-Develop:** The extensive class libraries make it simple to develop numerous functionalities. C# has influenced most of the world's programmers and has a long history in the programming world.
- **Cross-Platform:** Our program will only execute properly if the system has the NET framework installed. This is the most critical C# prerequisite. This might also be an excellent chance for novice programmers to get their feet wet with the .NET framework.
- **Better Integration:** .NET applications will have better integration and interoperability with other NET technologies. C# is based on common language

runtime (CLR), making it simple to interface with components written in other languages (specifically, CLR-compatible languages).

- **More Understandable Coding:** The idea of get-set methods has been formalized, making the codes more legible. We also don't have to bother about header files in C#. Coding in C# would be worthwhile.
- **Scarcity of Options:** In the Microsoft stack, there is a tool for everything. So, we just match your needs to the tool and use it. That is why we propose C# as a beneficial language, especially for novices.
- **Programming Support:** In C# (.NET framework), you may purchase support from Microsoft, as opposed to Java, where the community is our support. So, if something goes wrong, we may contact Microsoft for assistance.
- **Backward Compatibility:** .NET apps are only compatible with Windows systems, and Microsoft is discontinuing support for older Windows platforms. If we upgrade to a new version of Windows, you will always need to upgrade our .NET framework. This might be both a benefit and a drawback. A desire to continually improve motivates us to work hard and flourish in our area. This, in my opinion, is a positive thing.

CHAPTER 2

Setting Up Unity

In this chapter, we will be starting with the setup of Unity on our machines.

INSTALLATION AND CONFIGURATION

The fundamental need for creating content with Unity is to download the Unity engine and development environment. We may download extra modules for delivering to multiple platforms, as well as tools for integrating Unity scripting into Visual Studio, in addition to the main engine.

To get Unity, go to https://unity3d.com/get-unity/download.

Once there, select: Choose your Unity + Download.

DOI: 10.1201/9781003214755-2

On the following screen, under Personal, click the Try Now option. This is Unity's free alternative, which includes all of the key features. As we begin this course, it is preferable to understand how to utilize the engine before upgrading to Plus or Pro.

System Requirements for Unity Hub

Operating systems: Windows 7 SP1+, 8, 10, 64-bit only; Mac OS X 10.12+; Ubuntu 16.04, 18.04, and CentOS 7.

GPU: A graphics card that supports DX10 (shader model 4.0).

- Run the installation that we downloaded.
- Accept the license and terms, and then press the Next button.
- Select the components we want to install with Unity and then click "Next." Please keep in mind that we may always re-run the installation if we wish to modify the components.
- We can alter the location where Unity will be installed or leave the default location and click "Next."
- We may see additional questions before installation, depending on the components we choose. Follow the on-screen instructions and then click "Install." It may take some time to install Unity. Unity will be installed on our computer after the installation is complete.

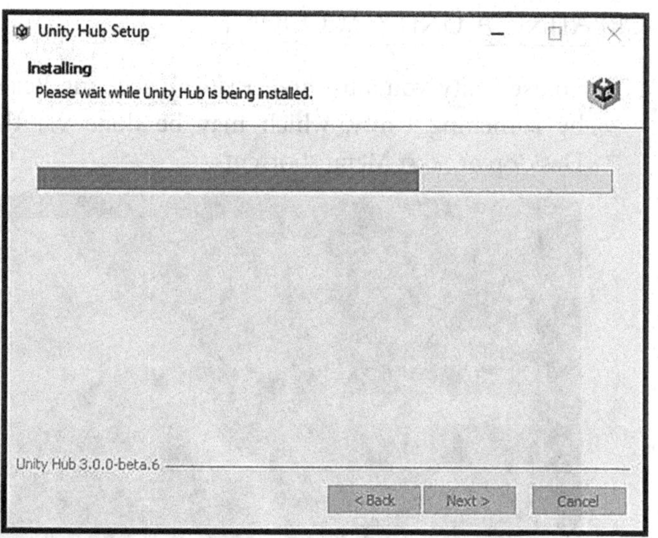
Unity Hub Setup
Installing
Please wait while Unity Hub is being installed.
Unity Hub 3.0.0-beta.6
< Back
Next >
Cancel

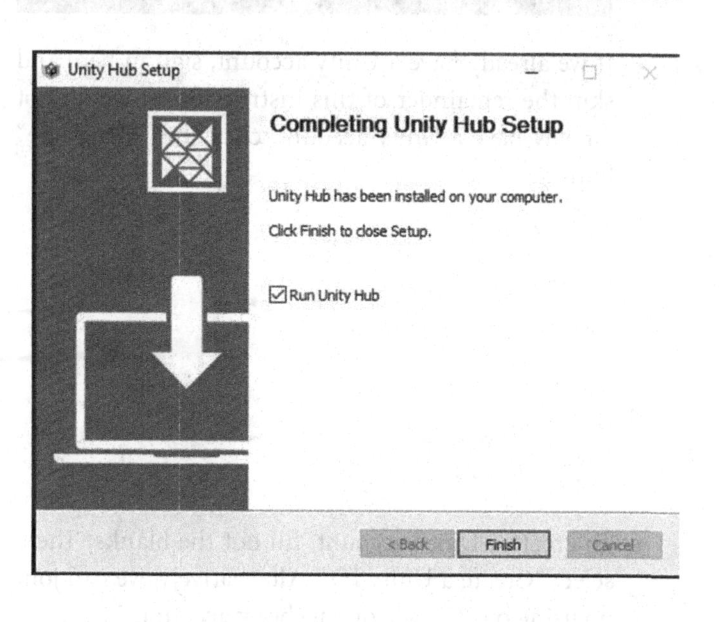
Unity Hub Setup
Completing Unity Hub Setup
Unity Hub has been installed on your computer.
Click Finish to close Setup.
Run Unity Hub
< Back
Finish
Cancel

CREATING A UNITY ACCOUNT

- To use Unity, you must first create an account. Begin by launching Unity, which may be done via the Desktop or Start Menu shortcuts.

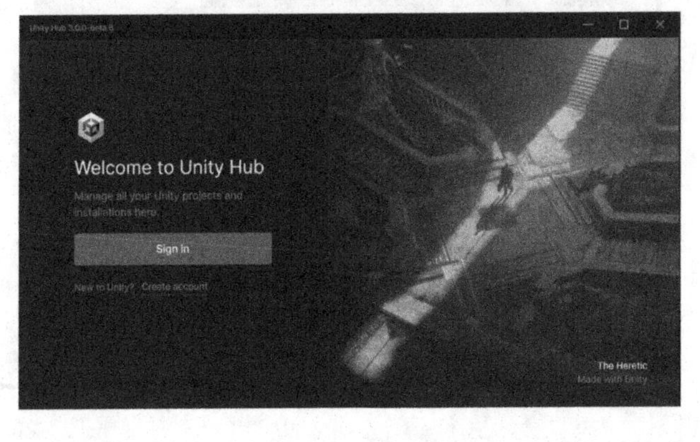

- If we already have a Unity account, sign in here and skip the remainder of this instruction. If we do not already have a Unity account, click the "create one" button.

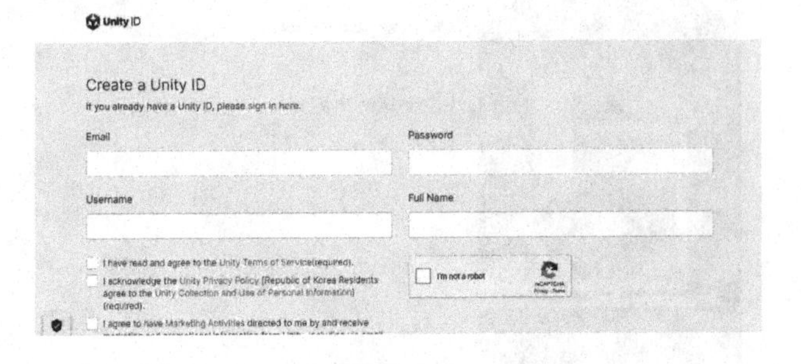

- To create a Unity account, fill out the blanks. Then, select "Create a Unity ID." Alternatively, we can join up using our Google or Facebook account.

- The email account we used to sign up for a Unity ID will receive a confirmation email. To confirm our email address, click the "Link to Confirm Email" button.
- After verifying our email, return to the Unity application and select "Continue."
- Click "Next" after selecting "Unity Personal."

DEVELOPING YOUR FIRST PROJECT

- Unity works well for both two-dimensional (2D) and three-dimensional (3D) games. From the Startup Screen, all Unity games begin as Projects.
- Launch the newly installed Unity; existing projects will appear in the hazy area.
- As illustrated above, the New icon is located in the upper-right corner of the window. When we click the button, we will be sent to the Project Setup screen.
- We may give our project a name, choose where it will be saved, the type of project, and add existing assets.
- For the time being, let's call our first project "Hello World!" and set it to 2D mode.
- Click Create Project to allow Unity to create your project's core files. This may take some time depending on our computer's performance, pre-added assets, and Project type.
- Once our new project has been created, and Unity has been launched.

- Let's take a quick look at what's visible in this window. For the time being, we are focused on four primary areas:
  - This is the window where we will create our Scenes. Scenes are the stages in which our game takes place. If we click on the tiny Game tab, we'll get a preview window that shows how the game will seem to the player. For the time being, it should have a plain blue backdrop.
  - The Inspector lives in this location. For the time being, it is empty because there are no items in our scenario. We'll see how the Inspector is used in the future.
  - The Scene Hierarchy is displayed in this window. It shows a list of all the objects in your currently active scene, along with their parent–child hierarchy. We will be adding things to this list shortly.
  - Finally, the Project Assets window is located in this section. All assets in our current project are saved and preserved in this folder. Externally imported assets, including textures, fonts, and sound files, are saved here before being utilized in a scene.

HOW DOES UNITY WORK?

All gaming in Unity takes place in scenes. Scenes are levels in which all components of our game occur, including gaming levels, the title screen, menus, and cut scenes.

A new Scene in Unity will contain a Camera object named the Main Camera by default. It is possible to add numerous cameras to the scene, but we will deal with the primary camera for the time being.

The primary camera depicts what it observes or "captures" in a space known as the viewport. Everything that enters this zone is visible to the player.

By placing our mouse inside the scene view and scrolling down to zoom out the scene view, we can see this viewport as a gray rectangle. (We may also accomplish this by holding Alt and dragging the Right-click button.)

A scene is composed of items known as GameObjects. GameObjects can range from the player's model to the screen's graphical user interface (GUI), from buttons and adversaries to unseen "managers" such as sound sources.

GameObjects are associated with a set of components that explain how they behave in the scene and how they relate to others in the scene.

We can look into it right now. Look at the Inspector by clicking on the Main Camera in the Scene Hierarchy. It will no longer be empty; instead, it will include several "modules."

The Transform component is the most critical component of any GameObject. Any item in a scene will have a transform that describes its position, rotation, and scale about the game world or, if applicable, its parent.

By clicking Add Component and choosing the required component, we may attach more elements to an object. In the following tutorials, we will also connect Scripts to GameObjects to give them programmed behavior.

Consider the following examples of components:

- **Renderer:** The person or program in charge of rendering and making items visible.
- **Collider:** Specifies the physical collision bounds for objects.
- **Rigidbody:** Provides an object with real-time physics attributes like weight and gravity.
- **Audio Source:** Provides object characteristics for playing and storing sound.
- **Sounds Listener:** This component "hears" audio and sends it to the player's speakers. One is present by default in the primary camera.
- **Animator:** This allows an item to interact with the animation system.
- **Light:** Causes the item to function as a light source with a range of effects.

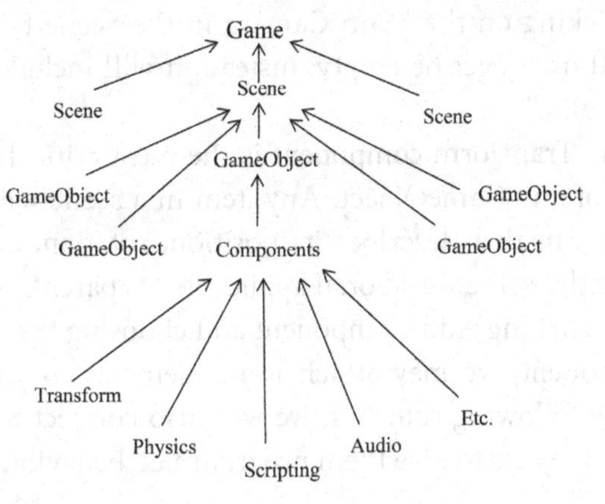

In this diagram, we can see how Unity composes itself into scenes using GameObjects.

CREATING SPRITES IN UNITY

- Sprites are basic 2D objects with graphical graphics (called textures) on them.
- When the engine is in 2D mode, sprites are used by default. Because sprites have no Z-width, they seem paper-thin when seen in 3D space. Unless turned in 3D space, sprites always face the camera at a perpendicular angle.
- When Unity creates a new sprite, it employs the utilization of a texture.
- This texture is then transferred to a new GameObject, subsequently attached to a Sprite Renderer component. This renders our gameObject apparent with our texture and gives it properties that control how it displays on screen.
- To make a sprite in Unity, we must first provide a texture to the engine.
- Let's start by making our texture. Select a typical image file, such as a PNG or JPG, save it, and drag the picture into Unity's Assets section.
- Drag the picture from the Assets folder into the Scene Hierarchy. We'll see that as soon as we let go of the mouse button, a new GameObject with the name of our texture appears in the list.

- While creating a sprite, keep the following points in mind:
    - We are adding an Asset to Unity by dragging it from an external source.
    - Because this Asset is an image, it gets converted to a texture.
    - By sliding this texture into the scene hierarchy, we create a new GameObject and a Sprite Renderer to the same name as our texture.
    - This sprite renderer draws the picture in the game using that texture. In our scenario, we've now included a sprite.

CHANGING SPRITES IN UNITY

The sprite we just imported may also be altered in a variety of ways to modify its appearance.

A toolbar may be seen in the upper left corner of the engine's interface.

Let us now go through the functionalities of buttons:

- The Hand tool is used to navigate about the scene without interfering with any of the items.
- Then there's the Move tool. This is used to move items around in the game environment.
- We have the Rotate tool in the middle, which allows us to rotate things together with the game world's Z-axis (or parent object).

- The Scaling tool is positioned to the right. This tool allows you to change the size (scale) of objects along specific axes.
- Finally, there is the Rect tool. This tool functions similarly to a combination of the Move and Scaling tools; however, it is prone to losing precision. It is more beneficial for organizing user interface (UI) components.

As the project's complexity grows, these tools become more valuable.

TRANSFORMS AND OBJECT PARENTING IN UNITY

When we first started, we spoke about how the transformation of a gameObject is likely its most significant component. In this chapter, we will go through the element in depth.

We will also be introduced to the notion of Object Parenting.

Transforms have three discernible properties: position, rotation, and scale. Each of them has three possible values for each of the three axes. When it comes to placement, 2D games often do not emphasize the Z-axis. The Z-axis is most commonly used in 2D games to create parallax.

The rotation attributes provide the amount of rotation (in degrees) an object has about that axis about the game environment or the parent object.

When relative to its original or native size, an object's scale determines how huge it is.

As an example, consider a square with dimensions of 2×2. If we scale this square by 3 against the X-axis and 2 against the Y-axis, we get a 6×4 square.

WHAT EXACTLY IS OBJECT PARENTING?

Objects in Unity follow a hierarchical architecture. GameObjects can become "parents" of other GameObjects using this mechanism.

When a GameObject has a parent, all transform modifications are performed about another GameObject rather than the game world.

For instance, an object with no parent placed at (10, 0, and 0) will be 10 units distant from the game globe's centre.

Nevertheless, a gameObject with a parent at (10, 0, 0) will consider the parent's current location to be the center.

It is as basic as dragging and dropping GameObjects onto the designated parent to parent them. A "child" item is represented in the object list by a small indentation and an arrow next to the parent object.

Parenting GameObjects have a variety of applications. For example, all of the numerous tank sections may be parented under a single GameObject named "tank."

As a result, when this "tank" parent GameObject moves, the entire pieces move with it since their location is continually updated according to their parent.

UNITY INTERNAL ASSETS

In addition to importing external assets from other applications such as audio files, photos, 3D models, and so on, Unity allows you to create internal assets. These assets are developed within Unity and do not require an additional application to create.

The following are some notable instances of internal assets:

- **Scenes:** These serve as "levels."
- **Animations:** These include information on the animations of a gameObject.
- **Materials:** These dictate how lighting influences an object's look.
- **Scripts:** This is the code that will be written for the gameObjects.
- **Prefabs:** These serve as "blueprints" for GameObjects, allowing them to be produced during runtime.

Placeholders, Sprites, and Models are also essential assets. These are used when we require rapid placeholder graphics and models to be updated later with actual graphics and models.

Right-click in the Assets folder and select Create to create an internal asset. We'll make a Triangle and a Square in this example. Scroll down to the Sprites section and pick Triangle.

Repeat for Square and you should have two new graphic assets.

SCENE SAVING AND LOADING IN UNITY

When we've completed a substantial amount of work, we'll want to save our progress. In Unity, using Ctrl + S will not save our project.

Everything in Unity takes place in scenes. Saving and loading are also required; we must save our current work as a scene (.unity extension) in our assets.

Let us put it to the test. If we press Ctrl + S and name our scene, we will see a new asset in our Assets area. The scene file may be found here.

Let's try to make a new scene now. To do so, go to the Assets menu and select Create - > Scene. Give our new scene a name and press the Enter key.

Scenes may be loaded into the editor by double-clicking them in the Editor mode (while the game is not running). When we load a scene with unsaved modifications on our current one, we will be prompted to save or discard our changes.

OUR VERY FIRST SCRIPT

Importing photos and having them stay motionless in our game will not get us very far. It could make a great picture frame, but it's not a game.

Scripting is required for creating games in Unity. Scripting is the process of authoring blocks of code that are attached to GameObjects in the scene like components. Scripting is among the most effective tools at our disposal, with the ability to make or break a good game.

Scripting in Unity is done using either C# or Unity's JavaScript implementation, known as UnityScript (although, with the 2018 cycle, UnityScript is currently entering its deprecation phase; therefore, it is not recommended to utilize it). We'll be using C# for the rest of this series.

To make a new script, right-click in the Assets folder and select Create -> C# Script. We may also use the Assets tab in the engine's top bar.

A new asset should appear when we create a new script. For the time being, keep the name as it is, and double-click it.

Along with running the script, our default integrated development environment (IDE) should launch.

Let's take a closer look at what it is:

```
using System.Collections;
using System.Collections.Generic;
using UnityEngine;
public class NewBehaviourScript :
MonoBehaviour
{
// This should be used for startup
void Start()
{
}
// The update function is called once each
frame
void Update()
{
}
}
```

Our script name will appear as a class deriving from MonoBehaviour. What exactly is MonoBehaviour? It is an extensive collection of classes and methods. It aids in the development of all scripts in Unity in one way or another. The more programs that create in Unity, the more we'll discover how helpful MonoBehaviour is.

As we continue, we have two private scripts with no return types, notably the Start and Update procedures. The Start function is called once for the first frame that the gameObject on which it is called is active in the scene.

Following the Start function, the Update method executes each frame of the game. Usually, Unity games run at

60 FPS (frames per second), which means the Update function is called 60 times every second while the item is active.

You may use Unity scripting to access the full MonoBehaviour class, as well as key C# functionality like generic collections, lambda expressions, and XML parsing, to mention a few.

BASIC MOVEMENT SCRIPTING IN UNITY

Based on the user's input, we will develop code that causes a gameObject to move up, down, left, and right. It should make it easier for us to understand the Unity scripting workflow.

Keep in mind that each GameObject has at least one component—Transform. What's unique about a gameObject's Transform is that it appears as a variable on Unity's scripting side, allowing us to manipulate it using code. This is not limited to the Transform; all components in Unity have attributes that may be accessed via variables in scripting.

Let's begin with the movement script. Make a new script and call it "Movement."

Now, launch the script, and you should see the same information as in the previous lesson.

Let's make a speed public float variable. Creating a variable public in Unity has several benefits:

> The variable appears as an editable field within the editor, eliminating the need to modify the values in code manually.

```
public class Movement: MonoBehaviour
{
public float speed;
}
```

This script should compile in Unity if we save it without touching the other functions.

Then, from the Assets, drag and drop the script onto the GameObject. If we do it right, we should see the GameObject's properties.

We may use the update() function instead of start() since the speed value is configurable and does not need to be modified in code all the time ().

Consider the following goals for the Update method:

- Examine for user-input.
- Read the input directions if there is any.
- Change the transform of the item's position values based on its speed and direction. We will use the following code:

```
void Update()
{
float hi = Input.
GetAxisRaw("Horizontal");
float vi = Input.GetAxisRaw("Vertical");
gameObject.transform.position = new
Vector2 (transform.position.a + (hi *
speed), transform.position.b + (vi *
speed));
```

Let us now quickly go through the code.

First, we create a floating-point variable called hi (for horizontal), whose value is determined by the Input.

The GetAxisRaw method. Depending on the player's key hit on the up/down/left/right arrows, this function returns –1, 0, or 1.

The Input class is in charge of receiving user input in the form of key presses, mouse input, controller input, etc. The GetAxisRaw technique is a little more challenging to grasp, so we'll return to it later.

The location of our gameObject is then updated to a new point determined by constructing a new Vector2. The Vector2 requires two arguments, which are the x and y values. We supply the total of the object's current location and speed for the x value, thereby adding some amount to its position every frame the key is pushed.

Return to Unity and save this script. Unity will automatically update all scripts after a successful build, so we won't have to reattach the script repeatedly.

After that, alter the value of the speed in the GameObject's attributes to 0.8. This is significant since a greater number will lead the player to move too quickly.

Now, press the Play button to watch our first mini-game in action.

Try moving around using the arrow keys. Simply hit the Play button again to end the game. We can also change the speed in real time, so we don't have to stop and start the machine all the time.

UNDERSTANDING COLLISIONS IN UNITY

Collisions in Unity are detached from the real Sprite, connected as distinct components, and computed independently. Let us now investigate the reason behind this.

Every GameObject in your game is a GameObject. Even the individual tiles that comprise your level are GameObjects in their own right.

When we consider each component to be a GameObject, we see that there may be thousands of GameObjects in a scene, all interacting in some way.

If Unity introduced collisions to every single GameObject, it would be impracticable for the engine to compute collisions for every one of them.

We'll go ahead and construct a rudimentary "wall" against which our player character can collide. Create another sprite and scale it up with the Rect tool to do this. We'll additionally tint it red using the Color property of the Sprite Renderer component.

Now, in the Inspector, select Add Component and enter "Box Collider 2D." When you click the first component, a new one should emerge.

A bright green line will appear around the circumference of our GameObject. This is the point at which two objects collide. It determines the primary form of collidable items.

Repeat the process with our moveable GameObject.

Of course, collisions in Unity aren't only confined to boxes. They can take many different shapes and sizes, and they are not necessarily precise replicas of the object's attributes. They can also be polygonal in form.

It is relatively uncommon for developers and designers to employ approximate forms in collision borders to simplify colliders and eliminate extra engine computations. We'll soon learn how to use our colliders to make different shapes and sizes.

Now that we've established our collision limits, press play to see how it works. Our mobile item is not acting normally, as we will discover.

RIGIDBODIES AND PHYSICS IN UNITY

We will now change the values of the GameObject's position directly. We just add a value to the position when the player presses a key. We need a method to have the player move so that it responds appropriately to borders and other GameObjects.

To do so, we must first define rigidbodies. Rigidbodies are GameObject components that allow them to respond to real-time physics. This includes responses to forces and gravity, as well as mass, drag, and velocity.

Simply click Add Component and type Rigidbody2D into the search area to add a Rigidbody to your GameObject.

By selecting Rigidbody2D, we may link the component to our GameObject. We'll note that several more fields have opened up now that it's connected.

The GameObject will tumble vertically down owing to gravity if the default parameters are used. Set the Gravity Scale to 0 to avoid this.

Because the GameObject does not yet have anything to do with its physics component, there will be no observable difference when we play the game.

Let us reopen our code and rewrite it to address our problem:

```
public class Movement: MonoBehaviour
{
public float speed;
public Rigidbody2D body;
// Update function is called once each
frame
void Update()
{
```

```
float hi = Input.GetAxisRaw("Horizontal");
float vi = Input.GetAxisRaw("Vertical");
body.velocity = new Vector2(hi * speed, vi
* speed);
}
}
```

We can see that in the definitions, we reference a Rigidbody2D, and our update method uses that reference rather than the Object's transform. This signifies that the Rigidbody has now been assigned the task of moving.

Because we haven't set anything to the body reference, we may anticipate raising a NullReferenceException. If we compile and run the game as is, we will get the following error in the editor's bottom left corner.

Let's look at the component generated by the script to see how we can remedy this. Remember that public properties in Unity produce their fields.

Play the game after increasing the pace to roughly 5.

Our collisions will now function properly.

CUSTOM COLLISION BOUNDARIES IN UNITY

Let's begin with the Box Collider. The Box Collider (2D) is a rectangle with four movable sides. Click on the box in the Collider's component.

The collider will display four "handles." We may resize these handles by dragging them around.

Unity determines the best feasible match for the collider's form for basic shapes, assuming we select the correct one. Choosing the circle collider on a circle sprite, for example, will match it to its radius.

Unity will strive to construct the simplest yet most sophisticated collision form for increasingly complex shapes. We must use the Polygon Collider 2D for this.

Try clicking the Edit Collider button and experimenting with the colliders.

UNDERSTANDING PREFABS AND INSTANTIATION IN UNITY

During gaming, it is critical to be able to instantiate and delete objects. Instantiating simply implies bringing something into being. Items "spawn" in the game, adversaries die, GUI components disappear, and sceneries are loaded in game at all times. Knowing how to effectively get rid of unnecessary stuff and bring in those we do becomes even more important.

Let us first define prefabrication. Prefabs are thought to be essential for understanding how Instantiation works in Unity.

Prefabs are blueprints for GameObjects. Prefabs are, in some ways, a duplicate of a GameObject that may be formed and placed in a scene even if the GameObject did not exist at the time the scene was built; in other words, prefabs can be used to dynamically construct GameObjects.

Drag the relevant GameObject from our scene hierarchy into the project Assets to create a prefab. Now, in our script, we call the Instantiate() function to make a GameObject. This MonoBehaviour method accepts a GameObject as a parameter to determine which GameObject to create/duplicate. It also provides several overrides for modifying the transform of the freshly made object and parenting.

Let's see if we can make a new hexagon anytime we press the Space key. Make a new script called Instantiator and launch it. Enter the following code in the Update method. In this case, we're utilizing the Input class's GetKeyDown function to see if the player pushed a particular button during the previous frame. Because we want it to keep checking, we put it under Update, which runs 60 times per second. If the key supplied by the KeyCode enum (which specifies all possible keys on a conventional keyboard) is pressed in that frame, the GetKeyDown function returns true.

```
public class Instantiator: MonoBehaviour
{
public GameObject Hexagon1;
// The update function is called once each
frame
void Update ()
{
if (Input.GetKeyDown(KeyCode.Space))
{
Instantiate(Hexagon1);
}
}
}
```

The public GameObject declaration at the top generates a slot identical to our earlier courses for the Rigidbody2D. This slot, however, only takes prefabs (in editor time) and gameObjects (at runtime).

Save the script and wait for it to compile. After that, go to our object hierarchy's right-click menu and pick Create Empty to create a new, empty GameObject.

Give this Object a memorable name, such as Instatiator Object, connect our freshly constructed script to it. Drag the prefab we made into the slot that appears for the GameObject.

When we run the game now, hitting the Spacebar will generate a new Hexagon object similar to the one we used to construct the prefab. In the object hierarchy, we can watch each hexagon being generated. We can't see them in the game because they're all being made one after the other at the moment.

DESTRUCTION OF GAMEOBJECTS IN UNITY

It is just as crucial to destroy GameObjects as it is to create them. This session will teach us how to destroy GameObjects.

Thankfully, destroying GameObjects is as simple as creating them. All you need is a reference to the object to be destroyed and then call the Destroy() function with that reference as an argument.

Let us now attempt to create five hexagons that will self-destruct when a specific key is pushed.

Open Visual Studio and create a new script named HexagonDestroyer. To get started, we'll make a public KeyCode variable. A KeyCode is used to indicate a key on a standard keyboard, and it is utilized by the Input class in its methods. We can make this variable accessible through the editor by making it public like we did with Rigidbody and Prefabs earlier. When making the variable public, we don't need to hardcode values like "KeyCode.A" into the code. We can make the code as versatile as we like by including as many objects as we desire.

```
public class HexagonDestroyer: MonoBehaviour
{
public KeyCode keyToDestroy;
// The update function is called once each
frame
```

```
void Update ()
{
if (Input.GetKeyDown(keyToDestroy))
{
Destroy (gameObject);
}
}
}
```

Take a look at how we utilized the variable "gameObject" (small g, capital O) in the procedure.

This new gameObject variable (of type GameObject) refers to the gameObject this script is associated with. If we connect this script to many objects, they will all react the same way whenever this variable is present.

However, don't get them mixed up.

- The class GameObject with a capital G and O covers all GameObjects and offers basic methods such as Instantiate, Destroy, and ways to obtain components.
- The particular instance of a GameObject, marked by a small g and a capital O, refers to the gameObject with which this script is now attached.

Let's now build our code and return to Unity.

We'll now make a new hexagon sprite and link our script to it. Then, in the hierarchy, right-click the gameObject and select Duplicate. In the hierarchy, a new sprite is produced; use the Move tool to reposition it. Repeat the procedures to make more hexagons.

Examine the script components of each hexagon by clicking on it. We may now program a GameObject to destroy itself when a particular key is hit. For example, let's make five hexagons and program them to explode when the A, S, D, F, and G keys are pushed.

We may set the same key on numerous hexagons, and they will all destroy themselves at the same time when the key is hit; this is an example of the gameObject reference, which we can use to refer to particular objects using the script without having to set them separately.

The same key may be put on numerous hexagons, and they will all destroy themselves at the same time when the key is pushed; this is an example of how to utilize the gameObject reference, which we can use to refer to particular objects in the script without having to set them separately.

It is critical to realize that destroying a GameObject does not result in the object shattering or exploding. In terms of the game (and its programming), destroying an item simply (and instantly) ends its existence. The links to this object and its references are just no longer working, and trying to either access or use will usually result in errors and crashes.

COROUTINES IN UNITY

When creating games with Unity, the most valuable tools are coroutines. Consider the following piece of code to grasp better what coroutines are all about.

```
IEnumerator MyCoroutineMethod()
{
// code
yield return null;
}
```

In general, when we call a function in Unity (or C#, for that matter), the function will execute from beginning to end. In terms of your code, this is what you would consider "typical" behavior. However, there are occasions when we wish to purposefully slow down a function or make it wait for a more extended period than the split-second length that it runs for. A coroutine can do just that: a coroutine is a function that can wait and time its activity and pause it completely.

Look at some examples of how a coroutine works. Assume we want to create a square that alternates between red and blue at one-second intervals.

To begin, we'll make a sprite. Then, create a new script and call it ColorChanger.

We receive a reference to the Sprite Renderer of the sprite in this script. However, we shall obtain the component differently. Instead of drag and drop the component into a slot, we will ask the script to detect the element itself.

This is accomplished using the GetComponent function, which returns the first matching component found. We can use this function to automatically identify and obtain a reference to our renderer because we only utilize one Sprite Renderer per object.

Remember that the renderer is in charge of making the sprite visible on screen.

The renderer contains a color property that affects the sprite's global color; this value must be changed. Making the Color values public allows us to select them using the editor in our operating system's default color picker.

```
private SpriteRenderer srr;
public Color color1;
public Color color2;
```

```
void Start ()
{
srr = GetComponent<SpriteRenderer>();
StartCoroutine(ChangeColor());
}
IEnumerator ChangeColor()
{
while (true)
{
if (srr.color == color1)
sr.color = color2;
else
srr.color = color1;
yield return new WaitForSeconds(3);
}
}
```

Now we'll use a while loop to catch our coroutine function.

In C#, we simply construct a method that returns an IEnumerator to establish a coroutine. A yield return statement is also required. The yield return line is unique in that it informs Unity to pause the script and resume on the next frame.

There are several methods for yielding a return, one of which is to create an instance of the WaitForSeconds class. This causes the coroutine to pause for a certain number of real-world seconds before continuing.

Let's build our code and return to Unity. Select our alternating colors and press the play button. Our object should now alternate between the two colors at three-second intervals. We can also make the interval a public variable and vary the frequency of the color changes.

Coroutines are commonly used for timed procedures like the one we just accomplished. Each of the WaitForX methods has its own set of applications. Coroutines can also be used to execute "on the side" programs that run independently while the game is running. This is handy for loading off-screen elements of a vast level while the player starts at a specific location, for example.

THE CONSOLE IN UNITY

The Developer outputs will be read in the Console. These outputs can be used to quickly test bits of code that do not require further testing functionality.

In the default console, there are three categories of messages. Most compiler standards can be associated with these messages:

- **Errors:** Errors are problems or exceptions that prohibit the code from operating.
- **Warning Signals:** Warnings are defects that will not prevent your code from executing but may cause problems during execution.
- **Messages:** Messages are outputs that communicate information to the user; they seldom reveal concerns.

We may even instruct the Console to display our messages, cautions, and failures. We will make use of the Debug class.

The Debug class is a component of MonoBehaviour that provides methods for writing messages to the Console, much to how we would produce typical output messages in our beginning applications.

The Console may be found on the tab above the Assets region. The console's outputs are more valuable to the programmer than to the end user or player.

Let's send an important message to the Console. This will alert us if the Space key is pressed. We'll use the Log method for this, which accepts an Object as an argument, which we'll fill with a string.

We may start from scratch or edit an existing script.

```
void Update()
{
if (Input.GetKeyDown(KeyCode.Space))
Debug.Log("Space-key pressed!");
}
```

After we've saved, compiled, and ran this code (by connecting it to a GameObject, of course), try hitting the spacebar. Our message will be written out if we click on the Console tab.

Similarly, the LogWarning and LogError methods can be used to produce cautions and errors, respectively. These will be handy for testing tiny pieces of code without having to implement them.

INTRODUCTION TO AUDIO IN UNITY

There is a reason why audio is so important in games; it is essential for adding esthetic value to the game. From the first Pong, one can hear beeps and boops when the ball alternately hits the paddles. At the time, it was a very rudimentary short square wave sample, but what more could you ask from the grandfather of all video games?

Many factors influence how we hear sound in real life, including the speed of the item, the sort of context it is in, and the direction it is coming from. A variety of variables might place an undue strain on our engine. Instead, we attempt to imagine how our sound might operate in our game and then design around that.

This is especially noticeable in 3D games because there are three axes to contend with.

We have specialized audio perception and playback components in Unity. These elements work together to produce an effective sound system that feels natural in the game.

Unity offers a plethora of essential tools and effects, such as reverb, the Doppler effect, real-time mixing and effects, and so on.

Components of Audio

We will learn about the three essential audio components in Unity.

- **AudioSource:** The AudioSource component is the main component attached to a GameObject for it to play sound. It will playback an AudioClip when activated by the mixer, code, or when it awakens by default.

  An AudioClip is nothing more than a sound file that has been inserted into an AudioSource. It can be any standard audio file format, such as.mp3,.wav, or others. An AudioClip is also a component in and of itself.

- **AudioListener:** An AudioListener is a component that listens to all audio in the scene and sends it to the computer's speakers. It serves as the game's ears. All audio we hear is from the perspective of this AudioListener. For a scenario to operate correctly, just one AudioListener should be present. The Listener is tied to the primary camera by default. The Listener has no exposed attributes that the designer would be interested in.
- **Audio Filters:** Audio Filters can be used to modify the output of an AudioSource or the intake of an AudioListener. These are individual components that may alter the reverb, chorus, filtering, and so forth. Each filter comes as its component with accessible settings for fine-tuning how it sounds.

Making a Noise

Let's attempt to build a button that emits a sound when pressed. To begin, we will create a Circle sprite and color it red.

Let us now add an Audio Source to this sprite. We must provide a sound for the item for it to play one. Let's put this sound effect to good use:

https://orangefreesounds.com/ding-sfx/.

Drag the sound effect into the Assets folder.

When Unity imports this asset as a sound file, it converts it to an AudioClip automatically. As a result, we may drag this sound clip directly from the Assets to the Audio Clip slot in our sprite's Audio Source.

Remember to deselect "Play on Awake" in the Audio Source attributes after dragging the sound clip from the Assets straight onto the Audio Clip slot in our sprite's

Audio Source; otherwise, the sound will play the instant the game begins.

Let's get started with our coding. Make a new script called "BellSound" and launch it.

Because our Audio Source is controlled by code, we must first obtain a reference to it.

We'll utilize the GetComponent function again.

```
public class BellSound: MonoBehaviour
{
AudioSource mySource;
// for initialization Use this
void Start ()
{
mySource = GetComponent<AudioSource>();
}
```

Let us now put up the technique for detecting the object that has been clicked. MonoBehaviour provides us with the method we require, OnMouseDown. When the mouse is within the range of a collider of that gameObject, the function is invoked.

Let us connect a collider to our button now because we haven't done so yet.

We won't require a Rigidbody for this one nor will we need to access it via code. It only needs to be present for the procedure to operate.

Let us put the approach to the test and see whether it works. Add the following code to our script and link it to the button.

```
void OnMouseDown()
{
Debug.Log("Click");
}
```

Play the game after saving and attaching the script. When we click the button, a message should appear in the Console.

We are now one step closer to hearing the sound. All that remains is to invoke the Play method on the Audio Source object.

```
void OnMouseDown()
{
mySource.Play();
}
```

Save your script and execute it in the game. When we press the button, we should hear the sound play.

STARTING WITH THE UI IN UNITY

This session will teach about the design process for UI components in Unity. This provides the basic setup as well as an overview of the common Unity parts.

The approach for designing UI in Unity differs somewhat from the one we've been following thus far. To begin with, UI components are not normal GameObjects and hence cannot be utilized as such. UI elements are created differently; for example, a menu button that looks correct in a 4:3 resolution may appear stretched or deformed in a 16:9 screen if not correctly set up.

In Unity, UI components are not immediately put on the scene. They are constantly added as children of a particular GameObject known as the Canvas. The canvas serves as a "drawing sheet" for the scene's UI, where all UI components are rendered. Without an existing Canvas, creating a UI element from the Create context menu will produce one for us.

Let's have a look at the Canvas GameObject now to learn about the new components:

The Rect Transform at the top looks to contain a slew of additional features that a conventional GameObject's Transform lacks.

Whereas the Transform of a standard GameObject represents an imaginary point in 3D space, the RectTransform specifies an imaginary rectangle. This implies we'll need more attributes to determine where the rectangle is, how wide it is, and how it's orientated.

We can see several conventional rectangle attributes like Height and Width and two new Anchor properties.

Anchors are spots on the Canvas that other things can "lock" onto. This implies that if a UI element (say, a button) is attached to the Canvas on the right, resizing the Canvas will keep the Button on the relative right of the Canvas at all times.

By default, we will not be able to change the shape of the canvas area, which will be a colossal rectangle around our scene.

The Canvas Component comes next. This is the master component, which has a few global parameters for how the UI is rendered.

The Render Mode is the first choice we encounter. This property specifies the mechanism for drawing the Canvas onto the game's display.

In the dropdown menu, we have three possibilities. Let us learn about the possibilities in the parts that follow.

- **Overlay for Screen Space:** This is the most common mode for menus, HUDs, and so on. It renders the UI on top of everything else in the scene, exactly as it is laid out and without exception. It also adjusts the UI elegantly as the size of the screen or game window changes. This is Canvas's default Render Mode.

- **Camera Screen Space:** The camera produces an imagined projection plane a predetermined distance away from the camera and projects everything UI onto it. This implies that the look of the UI in the scene is highly influenced by the camera settings, such as perspective, the field of view, and so on.
- **World Space:** UI elements act in World Space mode as if they were regular GameObjects put in the world. Because they are similar to sprites, they are often employed as part of the game world rather than for the player, such as in-game monitors and displays. Because of this, we may change the settings of the Canvas RectTransform directly in this mode.

The Canvas Scaler is a set of settings that allows us to alter the scale and look of UI components; it will enable us to specify how UI elements resize themselves when the size of the screen changes.

For example, UI components can be the same size independent of and in proportion to the screen size, or they can scale following a Reference Resolution.

The Graphics Raycaster is mainly responsible for raycasting (link to Unity Documentation for Raycasting) the UI components and ensuring that user-initiated activities like clicks and drags function properly.

THE BUTTON OF UNITY

We'll learn how to add UI components to our scene and how to operate with them.

Let us begin with a Button. To add a button, right-click anywhere in the Scene Hierarchy and select Create -> UI -> Button. If we don't already have a Canvas and an EventSystem, Unity will build one for us and set the button within the Canvas.

Remember that the size of the Canvas is independent of the size of the camera in Overlay rendering mode, which is the default mode. We may try it out by going to the Game tab.

When we play the scenario, we'll note that the button already has standard functionality, such as detecting mouse hover and changing color when pressed.

To be helpful in the UI, a Button must have functionality. Its attributes can be used to implement this capability.

Let's make a new script called ButtonBehaviour:

```
public class ButtonBehaviour: MonoBehaviour
{
int a;
public void OnButtonPress()
{
a++;
Debug.Log("Button clicked " + a + "
times.");
}
}
```

We created a simple technique that records how many times we pressed the button.

Let's start with a blank GameObject and connect this script to it. We do this because a button does nothing on its own; it simply calls the function defined in its scripting.

Now, navigate to the Button's properties and look for the OnClick() property.

When we click the Plus icon on the bottom tab, a new entry should appear in the list.

This item specifies which object the button click affects and which function of that object's script is invoked. Because of the event mechanism utilized in the button push, we can add more functions to the list to activate them.

Navigate to the No Function dropdown menu and choose our OnButtonPress method.

(Remember that we may call it whatever you wish; OnButtonPress is just a predefined naming convention.) It should be in the ButtonBehavior section.

If we play the game now, we may test the button, and the console will tell us how many times you pressed it.

TEXT ELEMENT IN UNITY

Even if more powerful and efficient community-built elements overtake it, Unity's inherent text UI is a beautiful starting place for beginners to get started developing UI.

For our purposes, the default Text element is more than adequate.

The fact that text is a unique UI element on its own is primarily due to its dynamism. Printing the player's current score to the screen, for example, requires the numeric value of the score to be converted to a string, often using the .toString() function.

To add a Text UI element, navigate to the Scene Hierarchy and select Create -> UI -> Text.

In your Canvas area, a new Text element should appear. When we look at its attributes, we can see that it has several beneficial choices.

The Text box, on the other hand, is the most important. We can put whatever we want the text box to say in that field, but we'd want to go a step farther.

To alter the font of the text, first, import the font file from your computer as an Asset into Unity. A typeface does not need to be explicitly tied to anything in the scene and maybe accessed straight from the Assets.

The Text element may also be accessible via scripting, emphasizing the significance of dynamic UI.

```
using UnityEngine;
using UnityEngine.UI;
public class ButtonBehaviour: MonoBehaviour
{
int a;
public Text myText;
public void OnButtonPress()
{
a++;
myText.text = "Button clicked " + a + "
times.";
}
}
```

The first modification we made was to create a new namespace reference. We include using UnityEngine.UI line because this reference is utilized to deal with Unity's UI components.

Following that, we establish a public Text variable to drag and drop our Text UI element.

Finally, we use myText.text to get at the text that this UI element holds.

If we save our script, we will notice a new slot in our ButtonManager for the Text UI element. Drag and drop the gameObject containing the Text element into the slot, then press the Play button.

THE SLIDER IN UNITY

We will learn about the last UI element. The Slider is frequently used when a value must be set between a maximum and lowest value pair. One of the most typical applications for this is to control audio volume or screen brightness.

To make a slider, navigate to Create -> UI -> Slider. On our scene, a new Slider element should appear.

If we go to the Slider's properties, you'll discover a slew of customization possibilities.

Let's see if we can build a volume slider out of this slider. To do so, open the ButtonBehaviour script (rename the ButtonManager GameObject as it is doing more than simply managing a button now) and include a reference to the Slider. We'll also tweak the code a little further.

```
public class ButtonBehaviour:
MonoBehaviour
{
int a;
public Text myText;
public Slider mySlider;
```

```
void Update()
{
myText.text = "Current Volume: " +
mySlider.value;
 }
}
```

Understand how we're utilizing the Update method to keep the value of myText.text updated.

Check the "Whole Numbers" box in the slider settings and set the maximum value to 100.

We will change the color of the text using its attributes to make it more noticeable.

Let us repeat the process of dragging the Slider GameObject onto the new slot and pressing play.

We are strongly advised to study and experiment with the other UI controls to discover which ones operate in which method.

MATERIALS AND SHADERS IN UNITY

In this section, we will study a bit of material and shaders. We'll start a new 3D project instead of our present 2D one to make things more transparent. This will make it easier for us to notice the numerous changes.

After we've created the new project, go to the Hierarchy, right-click, and select 3D Object -> Cube. This will place a new cube in the scene's center. In the Scene View, we may look around the cube by right-clicking and dragging the mouse. We may also use the scroll wheel to zoom in and out.

Now, click on the cube and examine its attributes.

The attribute at the bottom looks to have a Default material and a Standard shader.

What Exactly Is a Material?

A Material in Unity (and many other elements of 3D modeling) is a file that holds information on the lighting of an item with that material. Take note of how a gray sphere represents the material with some light streaming in from the top.

Don't be misled by the name; a Material has nothing to do with mass, collisions, or physics in general. A material defines how illumination affects an item made of that material.

Let us attempt to make our substance. Right-click in the Assets section, select Create -> Material, and call it "My Material."

These qualities are unlike anything we've seen before. This is because they are shader-programmed attributes rather than material-programmed properties.

The materials that your products are made of are what make them visible in the first place. Even in 2D, we employ a specific material that doesn't require as much illumination. Of course, Unity produces and applies it to everything, so we aren't even aware of its presence.

What Exactly Is a Shader?

A shader is software that determines how every pixel on the screen is rendered. Shaders are not written in C# or any other object-oriented programming (OOPS) language. They are written in GLSL, a C-like language that can send direct instructions to the GPU for quick processing.

THE PARTICLE SYSTEM IN UNITY

Particle Systems aid in the efficient generation of a large number of particles with short lifetimes. These systems have their rendering mechanism and can spawn particles even when hundreds or thousands of objects.

In the Particle System, particles are an ambiguous phrase; a particle is any particular texture, material instance, or object formed by the particle system. These aren't necessarily dots floating around in space (though they could be!), and they may be employed in various contexts.

A GameObject maintains a Particle System with the Particle System component connected; particle systems do not require any Assets to set up; however, various materials may be necessary depending on the effect you desire.

To make a particle system, use the Add Component option to add the Particle System component, go to the Hierarchy and select Create -> Effects -> Particle System. This will create a new GameObject that includes the particle system.

When we examine the Particle System's characteristics, we will notice that it comprises several modules. Only three modules are active by default: Emission, Shape, and Renderer. Other modules can be accessed by clicking the little circle next to their names.

We may see a little black arrow to the right of some numbers. This gives us more control over the values of individual particles. For example, we may instruct the Particle System to depict different sized, random particles like a water hose by setting the Start Size to Random Between Two Constants.

USING THE ASSET STORE IN UNITY

The Asset Store is one of Unity's most potent assets in the game engine industry; it contains a significant number of assets, tools, scripts, and even complete prepackaged projects that we may download.

We must have a valid Unity ID to utilize the Asset Store. If we don't already have one, we can make one on the Unity website.

After creating a Unity ID, go to the Asset Store tab, which is in the same row as the Scene View.

When we log in, you should be able to see our username in the upper right corner.

We'll import the Survival Shooter Tutorial project in this example. To do so, we'll look for it in the tab and then click on the asset released by Unity.

We'll click Download and wait for it to finish. The Download button will change to Import; click it again to add our new Asset to the currently active project when it's done.

A new window will appear, showing the contents of the newly imported Asset.

Depending on what we downloaded, this may be a single file, a group of files, or an entire tree containing folder and file hierarchies. When you press the Import button in Unity, it will automatically import all asset components, precisely what we want. Now, let's let Unity do its thing by clicking Import.

Attempting to download materials without paying for them is against the law, and there is always the risk of viruses, problems, or a lack of updates.

CHAPTER 3

Working with Scenes and GameObjects

Having installed Unity, we will be starting with scene management in this chapter.

WHAT ARE SCENES?

In Unity, scenes are where you work with the material. They are assets that contain the entirety or a portion of a game or program. For example, a primary game may be built in a single scene, but a more complicated game could require one scene per level, each setting, characters, obstacles, decorations, and user interface (UI). The number of scenes that can be included in a project is unlimited.

DOI: 10.1201/9781003214755-3

When we launch a new project for the first time, Unity displays an example scene with simply a Camera and a Light.

Scene Creation, Loading, and Saving

Let us start by scene creation and loading.

- **Creating a Scene:** There are various methods for making a new scene:
  - To create a new scene from a specified scene template, use the New Scene dialog.
  - Without accessing the New Scene dialog, use the menu or the Project window to create new scenes from your Project's Basic scene template.
  - Create a scene straight from a C# script using a specified template.

Using the New Scene dialog to create a new scene: Use the New Scene dialog to generate new scenes from specified scene templates in our Project. The New Scene dialog may also be used to identify and manage scene templates. See The New Scene dialog for more information.

The New Scene dialog appears by default when we create a new scene through the menu (File > New Scene) or by using a keyboard shortcut (Ctrl/Cmd + n).

To make a new Scene, follow these steps:

- Choose a template from the drop-down menu.
- Enable Load Additively if we want Unity to load the new scene additively.
- To make a new scene from the template, click Create.

If there are no cloneable dependencies in the template, Unity loads the new scene in memory but does not save it.

If the template contains cloneable dependencies, Unity invites us to save it to a place in the Project. Unity produces a folder with the same name and location as the new scene when we save the scene. The cloneable dependencies are then copied into the new folder, and the new scene is updated to use the cloned assets rather than the original assets used by the template scene.

- **Using the Menu to Create a New Scene:** To create a new scene without activating the New Scene dialog, use the menu (Assets > Create > Scene).

When we select New Scene from the menu, Unity copies the project's Basic template and adds it all to the folder that is now open in the application window.

- **Using the Project Window to Create a New Scene:** Use the menu bar in the Project window to make a new scene without opening the New Scene dialog.

Navigate to the folder in which we wish to save the new scene.

Select Create > Scene from the context menu by right-clicking the folder in the left-hand pane or an empty space in the right-hand pane.

When creating a new scene from the menu, Unity replicates the project's Basic template and adds the new scene to the folder we specify.

- **Creating a New Scene from a C# Script:** Use the Instantiate function to generate a new scene from a C# script that uses a specific scene template.

```
Tuple < Scene, SceneAsset >
SceneTemplate.
Instantiate(SceneTemplateAsset
sceneTemplate, bool loadAdditively,
string newSceneOutputPath = null);
```

The Instantiate function creates a new scene based on a scene template. It returns the newly formed Scene handle as well as the SceneAsset that corresponds to it. This scenario may be created in an additive manner. If the scene contains assets that must be cloned, we must specify a location for Unity to save the scene to disc.

- **New Scene Events:** When we create a new scene using a template, either through a script or by using the New Scene dialog, Unity generates an event. Unity triggers this event once the template is instantiated and after the EditorSceneManager.newSceneCreated and EditorSceneManager.sceneOpened events.

```
public class SceneTemplate1
{
public delegate void NewTemplateInstan
tiated(SceneTemplateAsset
sceneTemplateAsset, Scene scene,
SceneAsset sceneAsset, bool
additiveLoad);
```

```
public static event
NewTemplateInstantiated
newSceneTemplateInstantiated;
}
```

- **Scenes Are Being Loaded:** Start a scene by doing one of the following:
  - Double-click the scene asset in the Project window.
  - Choose File > New Scene from the menu.
  - Select File > Recent Scenes > [NAME-OF-SCENE] from the menu.

  If we have unsaved modifications in our current scene, Unity will urge us to save the scene or delete the changes.
- **Opening Several Scenes at the Same Time:** We can edit numerous scenes at the same time.
- **Saving Scenes:** Choose File > Save Scene from the menu, or press Ctrl + S (Windows) or Cmd + S (Mac) to save the scene we're now working on (macOS).

Multi-Scene Editing

This feature allows us to have numerous scenes open in the editor simultaneously, making it easier to handle scenes at runtime.

The option to access several scenes in the editor allows us to construct massive streaming worlds and enhances efficiency while working on scene editing together.

This session will go over:

- The Editor's multi-scene editing integration.
- The application programming interface (APIs) for Editor scripting and Runtime scripting.
- Current concerns that are known.

Select Open Scene Additive from the menu that displays for a scene asset in the editor, or dragging one or even more scenes from the Project window into the Hierarchy Window to open new scene and add it to the most recent list of scenes in Hierarchy.

When we have many scenes open in the editor, the hierarchy pane displays the contents of each scene separately. The contents of each scene are shown behind a scene divider bar that displays the scene's name and saves state.

Scenes can be loaded and unloaded while they are present in the hierarchy to expose or conceal the gameobjects stored inside each scene. This is not the same as adding or deleting them from the hierarchy pane.

If we have many scenes loaded, the scene dividers can be compressed in the hierarchy to the scene's contents, which may assist us in traversing our hierarchy.

When working on several scenes, each updated scene must have its changes saved; therefore, numerous unsaved scenes can be viewed simultaneously. In the scene divider bar, scenes with unsaved changes will have an asterisk next to the name.

The context menu in the divider bar allows us to save each Scene independently. Saving changes to all open scenes is as simple as selecting "Save Scene" from the file menu or hitting Ctrl/Cmd + S.

The menu bar in the scene divider bars allows us to do extra actions on the currently selected scene.

For loaded Scenes, the Scene divider menu appears:

- **Set Active Scene:** This allows us to choose the scenario in which new Game Objects are created/instantiated. One scene must always be designated as the current scene.
- **Save Scene:** Only the modifications to the specified scene are saved.
- **Save Scene As:** Saves the currently chosen scene (along with any current changes) to a new Scene asset.
- **Save All:** Changes to all scenes are saved.
- **Unload Scene:** The scene is unloaded, yet it remains in the Hierarchy window.
- **Remove Scene:** The scene is unloaded and removed from the Hierarchy window.
- **Select Scene Asset:** In the Project window, select the asset for the scene.
- **GameObject:** Provides a sub-menu for creating GameObjects in the specified scene. The menu replicates the items that may be created in Unity's main GameObject menu.

The Scene divider menu for unloaded Scenes is as follows:

- **Load Scene:** Loads the contents of the scene.
- **Remove Scene:** Take the scene out of the Hierarchy window.
- **Choose a Scene Asset:** In the Project window, select the asset for the scene.

Baking Lightmaps across Multiple Scenes

To bake Lightmap data for many scenes at once, open the scenes you wish to bake, disable "Auto" mode in the Lighting Window, and then click the Build button.

The lighting computations use static geometry and lights from all scenes. As a result, shadows and GI light bounces will operate in all scenarios. On the other hand, the lightmaps and real-time GI data are divided into data that is loaded and unloaded independently for each scene. Lightmaps and real-time GI data atlases are divided into scenes. This implies that lightmaps between scenes are never exchanged and may be securely emptied when a scene is unloaded.

At the moment, lightprobe data is always shared, and all lightprobes for all scenes baked together are loaded at the same time.

Alternatively, we may use the Lightmapping tool to automate the creation of lightmaps for various situations.

In an editor script, use the BakeMultipleScenes method.

Baking Navmesh Data with a Variety of Scenes

To bake navmesh data for numerous scenes at once, open each scene and click the Bake button in the Navigation

Window. The navmesh data will be integrated into a single object that all loaded scenes will share. The data is saved in the folder with the same name as the currently active scene (for example, ActiveSceneName/NavMesh.asset). This navmesh component will be shared by all loaded scenes. Save the impacted scenes after baking the navmesh to maintain the scene-to-navmesh reference permanently.

Alternatively, we may use the NavMeshBuilder.BuildNavMeshForMultipleScenes method in an editor script to automate the creation of navmesh data for numerous scenes.

Baking Data for Occlusion Culling with Several Scenes

To bake occlusion culling data for many scenes simultaneously, open the Scenes you wish to bake, open the Occlusion Culling window (menu: Window > Rendering > Occlusion Culling) and click the Bake button. The occlusion culling data is saved as an asset named OcclusionCullingData.asset in a folder named after the currently active scene. Assets/ActiveSceneName/OcclusionCullingData.asset, for example. In each open Scene, a reference to the data is added. Save the Scenes impacted after baking the occlusion culling data to make the Scene-to-occlusion-data reference durable.

If a Scene is loaded additively and has the same occlusion data reference as the current Scene, the occlusion data is used to initialize the static renderers and portals culling information for that Scene. Following that, the occlusion culling mechanism behaves as if all static renderers and portals had been baked into a single Scene.

Play Mode

In-Play mode, when there are several scenes in the Hierarchy, an additional scene called DontDestroyOnLoad will appear.

Prior to Unity 5.3, any objects constructed in Playmode and marked as "DontDestroyOnLoad" would stay in the hierarchy. These items are not considered part of any scene, but they are now presented as part of the unique DontDestroyOnLoad scene for Unity to display and for you to study.

The DontDestroyOnLoad scene is not accessible to us, and it is not available during runtime.

Scene-Specific Settings

Each scenario has its own set of settings. They are as follows:

Navmesh configuration Scene settings in the RenderSettings and LightmapSettings sections of the Occlusion Culling Window (both located in the Lighting Window)

Each scene manages its settings, and only the parameters connected with that scene are saved to the scene file.

If we have several scenes open, the rendering and navmesh settings from the active scene are utilized. This implies that if we wish to modify the settings of a scene, we must either open only one scene and do so or make the scene in question the active scene and do so.

When we change the current scene in the editor or during runtime, all of the settings from the new scene are applied and replace all prior settings.

Scripting

- **Scripting by an Editor:** We provide a Scene struct, an EditorSceneManager API, and a SceneSetup utility class for editor scripting.

The Scene struct is accessible both in the editor and at runtime, and it includes a few read-only values related to the scene itself, such as its name and asset path.

The EditorSceneManager class can only be found in the editor. It is derived from SceneManager and contains several methods to use editor scripting to accomplish all of the Multi Scene Editing functionality discussed above.

The SceneSetup class is a simple utility class that stores information about the current scene in the hierarchy.

Multiple scenes are now supported by the Undo and PrefabUtility classes. We may now use [PrefabUtility.InstantiatePrefab] to instantiate a prefab in a specified scene, and we can use (Undo.MoveGameObjectToScene) [ScriptRef:Undo.MoveGameObjectToScene]] to move objects to the root of a scene in an un-doable way.

- **Runtime Scripting:** The SceneManager class has methods for working with numerous scenes at runtimes, such as LoadScene and UnloadScene.

- **Remember:** The Save Scene As option in the File menu will only save the currently active scene. Save Scene will save all updated scenes and offer us to name the Untitled scene if one exists.

- **Tricks and Tips:** Holding Alt while dragging allows us to add a scene to the hierarchy while keeping it empty. This allows us to load the scenario later if necessary.

The Create option in the project window may be used to create new scenes. The default configuration of Game Objects will be used in new scenarios.

We may utilize EditorSceneManager to prevent setting up our hierarchy every time we restart Unity or make it easier to keep multiple settings.

Use GetSceneManagerSetup to retrieve a list of SceneSetup objects that describe the current configuration. We may then serialize these into a ScriptableObject or something else, along with any additional information about our scene setup that we wish to save.

To acquire the list of loaded scenes at runtime, use sceneCount and loop through the scenes using GetSceneAt.

GameObject.scene returns the scene to which a GameObject belongs, and (SceneManager.MoveGameObjectToScene).) moves a GameObject to the root of a scene.

It is best to avoid using DontDestroyOnLoad to persist management GameObjects that we wish to keep between scene loads. Instead, use SceneManager to construct a manager scene with all of your managers. SceneManager and LoadScene(path>, LoadSceneMode.Additive). To control our game progress, use UnloadScene.

Scene Templates

Unity replicates scene templates to generate new scenes. Consider a scene template to be a pre-configured scene with all of the stuff we wish to begin with. The Basic template, for example, generally includes a Camera and a light.

We can tailor the sorts of new scenes created in a project by creating our scene templates. Create templates for every level in a game for illustration, so everyone working on the project may begin their scenes with the appropriate materials and settings.

A template may be made from any Unity scene. After creating a template, we may use it to generate an unlimited number of new scenarios.

Creating Scene Templates

We may make a new scene template in one of three ways:

- Begin with an empty template.
- Make a template out of a pre-existing scene asset.
- Make a template out of the current scenario.

After creating a template, we may modify its properties or use it to build new scenarios.

Making a Blank Scene Template We may build blank scene templates and then customize them afterward. An empty template does not display in the New Scene dialog unless its attributes are edited to connect it with a scene asset.

To make an empty scene template in the current project folder, do the following:

- Select Assets > Create > Scene Template from the menu.

To create an empty scene template in a specific project folder, do the following:

Choose one of the following options:

- Right-click the folder in the Project window to open the context menu.
- Right-click the asset pane to access the context menu, then open the folder in the Project window.
- Choose to Create > Scene Template from the menu.

Making a Template from an Existing Asset in a Scene Any current scene may be converted into a scene template. After creating a template from an existing scene, we may wish to update its attributes to designate which of its dependencies Unity clones when creating a new scene from it.

To make a template from an existing scene asset, enter the Project window and choose one of the following options:

- To open the context menu, right-click a scene asset. Then go to Scene Templates > Create Scene Template From Scene.
- Select the scene asset, then choose Assets > Create > Scene Template From Scene from the main menu.

Making a Template Out of the Current Scene Select File > Save As Scene Template from the menu to generate a scene template from the current scene.

If we have any unsaved modifications, Unity will prompt us to save the scene before saving the template.

After creating a template from the current scene, we may wish to update its attributes to designate its dependencies on Unity clones when creating a new scene.

- **Creating Scene Templates from C# Scripts:** Scene templates may be created from C# scripts.

  Use the CreateSceneTemplate function to generate an empty scene template.

  ```
  SceneTemplate.CreateSceneTemplate(string
  sceneTemplatePath)
  ```

  Use the CreateTemplateFromScene function to construct a template from an existing scene. Unity connects the scene with the template and extracts the scene's dependencies automatically.

  ```
  SceneTemplate.CreateTemplateFromScene(
  SceneAsset sourceSceneAsset, string
  sceneTemplatePath);
  ```

Modifying Scene Templates

To edit a scene template, open it in an Inspector window after selecting it in the Project window.

The Inspector scene template has the following sections:

- **Details:** Specifies the scene the template will utilize and the template description that will display in the New Scene dialog.
- **Thumbnail:** This allows us to create a preview picture for the template.

- **Scene Template Pipeline:** Defines an optional custom script that will be executed when Unity builds a new scene from the template.
- **Dependencies:** They use the dependenciesdependencies** element in their manifests to specify the collection of packages they need. These are considered direct dependencies for projects but indirect or transitive dependencies for packages.

Details The Details section defines which scene to use as a template and how the template appears in the New Scene dialog.

Property	Description
Template scene	Specify which scene will be used as a template. This might be from any scenario in the Project.
Title	The name of the template. The name you provide here will be shown in the New Scene dialog.
Description	The description of the template. The explanation we put here will be shown in the New Scene dialog.
Pin in New Scene dialog	This setting determines whether or not this template gets pinned in the New Scene dialog. Pinned templates are always displayed at the top of the Scene Templates list in the Project list.

Thumbnail The Thumbnail section has choices for producing a template preview picture. In the New Scene dialog, the preview picture shows.

Property	Description
Texture	This property specifies a Texture asset to be used as a thumbnail for this template. In the Project, we may utilize any Texture asset. If we don't provide a Texture, the template will utilize the asset icon from the default scene template.
[Thumbnail Preview]	If the template contains a thumbnail texture, it will be shown.
Snapshot	This template has options for capturing a thumbnail picture.
View	Specifies whether the Main Camera view or the Game View should be captured.
Take Snapshot	To save the selected View, click this button.

Pipeline for Scene Templates To add a Scene Template Pipeline script to this template, use these settings.

A Scene Model When we build a new scene from a template, the pipeline script allows us to run custom code. See Customizing fresh scene creation for further information.

Dependencies This section includes all of the Dependencies for the template scene. When we build a new scene using the template, we may choose whether or not to clone each dependency.

To clone or reference a dependency, turn the Clone option on or off for each dependence in the list.

When we build a new scene from a template, Unity examines the template scene to see if it contains cloneable dependencies. If it does, Unity generates a folder with the same name as the new scene and stores any copied dependencies in it.

Customizing the Creation of New Scenes

Make a Scene Template Pipeline script and link it to the template to execute custom code whenever Unity creates a new scene from a template. Unity produces a new instance of the pipeline script every time you build a new scene from the template.

To link the script to a template, do the following:

- Edit the template's properties by inspecting it.
- Set the Scene Template Pipeline attribute to our Scene Template Pipeline script's path.

We may also link the script to the template using C# using the SceneTemplateAsset.templatePipeline function.

A Scene Template Pipeline script must be based on the [ISceneTemplatePipeline] or [SceneTemplatePipelineAdapter] interface. It should implement the events we wish to react to, such as BeforeTemplateInstantiation or AfterTemplateInstantiation in the code below.

Example:

```
using UnityEditor.SceneTemplate;
using UnityEngine;
using UnityEngine.SceneManagement;
public class
DummySceneTemplatePipeline1 :
ISceneTemplatePipeline
{
```

```
    public void BeforeTemplateInstantiat
ion(SceneTemplateAsset sceneTemplateAsset,
bool isAdditive, string sceneName)
    {
        if (sceneTemplateAsset)
        {
            Debug.Log($"Before Template
Pipeline {sceneTemplateAsset.name}
isAdditive: {isAdditive} sceneName:
{sceneName}");
        }
    }

    public void AfterTemplateInstantiati
on(SceneTemplateAsset sceneTemplateAsset,
Scene scene, bool isAdditive, string
sceneName)
    {
        if (sceneTemplateAsset)
        {
            Debug.Log($"After Template
Pipeline {sceneTemplateAsset.name} scene:
{scene} isAdditive: {isAdditive}
sceneName: {sceneName}");
        }
    }
}
```

The Sequence of Scene Template Instantiation

Unity executes multiple file actions when you build a new scene from a template with cloneable dependencies. The majority of these actions generate Unity events, which you can listen for and respond to in scripts.

The following is the instantiation sequence:

1. In the New Scene dialog, you select Create. Unity refers to the following:
   - The scene template is an asset.
     - **Scene Template:** This is the Unity Scene that corresponds to the template.
     - **A New scene:** This is a new instance of the Scene template.

   Unity triggers the ISceneTemplatePipeline. The template asset's BeforeTemplateInstantiation event ties the asset to an ISceneTemplatePipeline script that it activates.
2. Unity triggers the SceneTemplate.
3. The event NewTemplateInstantiating.
4. Unity generates a new scene that is a duplicate of the template scene.
5. Unity generates a folder named the same as the new scene and transfers all cloneable dependencies into it.
6. Unity loads the new scene into memory and sets off the following events:
   - EditorSceneManager.sceneOpening
   - MonoBehavior.OnValidate
   - EditorSceneManager.sceneOpened

7. Unity remaps all cloneable asset references, so the new scene refers to the clones.
8. Unity saves the new scene and causes the following actions to occur:
    - EditorSceneManager.sceneSaving
    - EditorSceneManager.sceneSaved
9. Unity triggers the ISceneTemplatePipeline.After-TemplateInstantiation for the template asset and binds the asset to an ISceneTemplatePipeline script that it triggers.
10. Unity triggers the SceneTemplate.NewTemplate-Instantiated event.

Settings for the Scene Template

Open the Project Options window (menu: Edit > Project Settings) and choose Scene Template from the category list to view the scene template Project settings.

New Scene Settings

The New Scene settings regulate what occurs when you create a new scene from the File menu (File > New Scene) or by using the Ctrl/Cmd + n keyboard shortcut.

Option:	Description:
New Scene menu	
New Scene dialog	The New Scene dialog box is being shown.
Built-in Scene	Without opening the New Scene dialog, this command creates a new scene. The new scene is a clone of the Basic template from the Project.

Types Settings by Default

The Default Types options determine whether Unity automatically clones particular types of assets when creating a new scene from a scene template.

Enable the Clone option for that asset type in the list to have Unity clone it by default.

Disable the Clone option for that asset type in the list to make Unity reference that asset type by default.

The Clone option for All Other Categories, whether enabled or disabled, sets the default clone/reference behavior for asset categories that do not appear in the list.

Click the Remove button to remove an asset type from the list.

To add an asset type to the list, do one of the following: In the Add-Type field, enter a specific asset type. Click the Browse button to start a search window to seek and select a particular asset type.

Then, to add the asset type to the list, click the Add button.

Click the Reset Defaults button to return to Unity's default asset type list and settings.

WHAT ARE GAMEOBJECTS?

The Unity Editor's most significant notion is the GameObject.

Every object in your game, from people and collectibles to lighting, cameras, and special effects, is a GameObject. A GameObject, on the other hand, cannot do anything on its own; it must be given characteristics before it can become a character, an environment, or a special effect.

Unity's primary objects are GameObjects, which represent characters, props, and scenery. They don't perform anything on their own, but they serve as containers for Components, which implement the functionality.

Components are used to provide a GameObject with the attributes it requires to become a light, a tree, or a camera.

We may add different combinations of components to a GameObject depending on the type of item we want to construct.

Unity includes a plethora of built-in component types, and we may even create our own using the Unity Scripting API.

A Light object, for example, is generated by connecting a Light component to a GameObject.

A solid cube object contains a Mesh Filter and Mesh Renderer element to depict the cube's surface and a Box Collider component to express the solid volume of the object in physics terms.

Specifications

A Transform component (which represents position and orientation) is constantly associated with a GameObject and cannot be removed. The additional components that provide the object's functionality can be added using the editor's Component menu or a script. There are also numerous helpful pre-constructed objects (basic shapes, Cameras, and so on) accessible under the GameObject > 3D Object menu; see Primitive Objects for more information.

Because GameObjects are such a vital element of Unity, there are a plethora of content manuals that go into great detail about them. More information on utilizing GameObjects in Unity may be found in the sections below.

- Transforms.
- Introduction to components.
- Primitive and placeholder objects.
- Using Components.
- Deactivating GameObjects.
- Tags.
- Creating components with scripting.
- Static GameObjects.
- Saving your work.

Transforms

The Transform is used to hold the position, rotation, scale, and parenting status of a GameObject and is thus highly significant. A Transform component is always associated with a GameObject; it is impossible to delete or construct a GameObject without one.

The Component of Transform

Each item in the scene. Every GameObject has a Transform that governs its Position, Rotation, and Scale.

Properties

Property:	Function:
Position	The Transform's position in X, Y, and Z coordinates.
Rotation	Rotation of the Transform in degrees around the X, Y, and Z axes.
Scale	The Transform's scale along the X, Y, and Z axes. The original size is represented by the value "1." (The size at which the object was imported).

A Transform's position, rotation, and scale values are all measured in relation to the Transform's parent. If there is no parent for the Transform, the attributes are measured in world space.

Transform Editing

Transforms can be controlled in three-dimensional (3D) space along the X, Y, and Z axes or two-dimensional (2D) space along the X and Y axes. These axes are represented in Unity by the colors red, green, and blue, respectively.

Transforms can be modified in the Scene View or by changing their attributes in the Inspector. Transforms in the scene may be modified using the Move, Rotate, and Scale tools. These tools may be found in the Unity Editor's top left-hand corner.

The tools are applicable to any item in the scene. When we click on an object, the tool gizmo will appear within it. The look of the gadget is determined by the tool picked.

When we click and drag on one of the three gizmo axes, its color will be yellow. The item will translate, rotate, or scale along the specified axis as we move the mouse. When we release the mouse button, the axis remains selected.

In Translate mode, there is also the ability to lock movement to a particular plane (i.e., allow dragging in two axes while keeping the third unchanged). The three little colored squares in the center of the Translate gizmo activate the lock for each plane; the colors correspond to the axis, which will be locked when the square is clicked(e.g., blue locks the Z-axis).

Parenting

When utilizing Unity, one of the most fundamental things to grasp is parenting. When a GameObject is the Parent of another GameObject, the Child GameObject moves, rotates, and scales the same way as its Parent. Parenting may be compared to the interaction between our arms and our body; anytime our body moves, our arms move as well. Child items can have their children, and so on. So our hands may be seen as "children" of our arms, with each hand having numerous fingers, and so on. There can be several offspring for each item, but only one parent. These several layers of parent–child interactions form a Transform hierarchy.

The root is the object at the very top of a hierarchy (e.g., the only item in the hierarchy that does not have a parent).

Drag any GameObject in the Hierarchy View onto another to create a Parent. The two GameObjects will form a Parent–Child connection as a result of this.

It's worth noting that the Transform values in the Inspector for any child GameObject are displayed relative to the Transform values of the Parent. These values are known as local coordinates. Returning to the analogy of the body and arms, our body's position may change while we walk, but our arms will remain attached at the same relative position. Working with local coordinates for child items usually is adequate for scene development. Still, gaming is frequently helpful to discover their actual position in world space or global coordinates. The Transform component's scripting API contains distinct properties for the local and global position, rotation, and scale and the ability to transform any point between local and global coordinates.

Non-Uniform Scaling Limitations

When the Scale in a Transform has distinct values for x, y, and z, this is referred to as non-uniform scaling (2, 4, 2). On the other hand, Uniform scaling has the same value for x, y, and z, for example (3, 3, 3). Non-uniform scaling can be advantageous in a few specific instances, although it introduces a few anomalies that uniform scaling does not:

- Some components do not entirely support Non-uniform scaling. Some features, such as the Sphere Collider, Capsule Collider, Light, and Audio Source, have a circular or spherical element specified by a radius attribute. In such circumstances, the circular shape will not become elliptical due to non-uniform scaling but instead, stay round.
- When a child item is rotated relative to a non-uniformly scaled parent, it may seem skewed or "sheared." Some components accept basic non-uniform scaling but do not function properly when skewed like this. A skewed Box Collider, for example, will not correctly match the form of the displayed mesh.

- A child object of a non-uniformly scaled parent will not have its scale automatically updated as it rotates for performance reasons. As a result, when the scale is ultimately updated, such as if the child object is disconnected from the parent, the child's form may appear to shift abruptly.

Scale's Importance

The Transform scale defines the difference in size between a mesh in your modeling application and a mesh in Unity. The size of the mesh in Unity (and hence the scale of the Transform) is critical, especially during physics modeling. The physics engine thinks that one unit in world space equals one meter by default. If an item is particularly enormous, it may appear to fall in "slow-motion"; the simulation is accurate since we see a vast thing fall a long distance.

The size of our item can be affected by three factors:

1. In your 3D modeling application, the size of our mesh.
2. The Mesh Scale Factor parameter in the Import Settings of the item.
3. Our Transform Component's Scale values.

We should not, ideally, change the Scale of your object in the Transform Component. The ideal method is to develop your models at a real-life scale so that we don't have to adjust the scale of our Transform. The next best approach is to change the scale at which your mesh is imported under our individual mesh's Import Settings. Specific optimizations occur based on the import size, and instantiating an object with a modified scale value might reduce speed.

Working with Transforms: Some Pointers

- It is helpful to set the parent's position to 0,0,0> before adding the kid when parenting Transforms. This implies that the kid's local coordinates will be the same as global coordinates, making it easy to ensure that the child is in the correct place.
- If we're going to use Rigidbodies for physics modeling, be sure to learn about the Scale property on the Rigidbody component reference page.
- The colors of the Transform axes (and other UI components) may be changed in the settings (Menu: Unity > Preferences, then pick the Colors & keys panel).
- The location of child morphs is affected by changing the Scale. Scaling the parent to (0,0,0) will, for example, place all children at (0,0,0) relative to the parent.

Components Are Introduced

A GameObject is a Unity Editor object that contains components. Components describe how a GameObject behaves.

This section explains how to see and interact with components in Unity and a quick overview of the most typical component settings.

To see a GameObject's components, pick it in the Scene or Hierarchy windows, then go to the Inspector window to get a list of its components and their settings.

Components can be interacted with directly in the Editor or via script. For information on how to control and interact with components using a script, see the Scripting section.

Configurations of Common Components

This section describes some of Unity's basic default component setups.

Component Transformation

In Unity, every GameObject has a Transform component. This component specifies the location, rotation, and scale of the GameObject in the game world and Scene view. This component cannot be removed.

The Transform component also supports the idea of parenting, which allows us to make a GameObject a child of another GameObject and control its position using the Transform component of the parent. This is a critical component of working with GameObjects in Unity.

Components of the Main Camera GameObject

Every new scene begins with a GameObject named Main Camera by default. This GameObject is set up to be the primary camera in our game. It includes the Transform component, the Camera component, and an Audio Listener for capturing audio in our application.

Making Use of Components

Components are the nuts and bolts of a game's objects and actions. They are the essential components of every GameObject. Before proceeding, read the GameObjects page if you do not yet grasp the link between Components and GameObjects.

A GameObject is a container for a variety of Components. By default, all GameObjects include a Transform Component. This is due to the Transform determining where the GameObject is positioned and how it is rotated and scaled. If the GameObject did not have a Transform Component, it would not have a position in the world. As an example, try making an empty GameObject now. Select GameObject->Create Empty from the menu. Examine the Inspector after selecting the new GameObject.

We can always use the Inspector to examine which Components are associated with the specified GameObject. The Inspector will always show you which Components are currently connected when they are added and deleted. The Inspector will be used to modify all of the characteristics of any Component.

Adding Components

The Components menu allows us to add Components to the specified GameObject. We'll give it a shot now by attaching a Rigidbody to the empty GameObject we just made. Select it and then go to the Component->Physics->Rigidbody menu. When we do this, the Rigidbody's characteristics will display in the Inspector. We can receive a surprise if you press Play while the empty GameObject is still chosen. Try it out and note how the Rigidbody has given the otherwise empty GameObject functionality. (The GameObject's transform's Y position begins to decrease. This is due to Unity's physics engine forcing the GameObject to fall under gravity.)

The Component Browser, which can be accessed via the Add Component button in the object's inspector, is another alternative.

The browser allows us to quickly traverse the components by category and also contains a search bar that we can use to find components by name.

A single GameObject can have any number or combination of Components attached to it. Some Components perform best when combined with others. The Rigidbody, for example, maybe used with any Collider. The NVIDIA PhysX physics engine controls the Rigidbody, and the Collider lets the Rigidbody collide and interact with other Colliders.

If we want to learn more about using a specific Component, we may do so by visiting the corresponding Component Reference page.

We may also view a Component's reference page from Unity by clicking on the small? in the Component's header in the Inspector.

Components Editing

Components' versatility is one of its best features. When we connect a Component to a GameObject, the Component has several values or Properties that may be changed in the editor when developing a game or by scripts while running the game. Properties are classified into two types: Values and References.

It's a blank GameObject with an Audio Source Component attached to it. All of the Audio Source settings in the Inspector are the defaults.

There is a single Reference property and seven Value properties in this Component. The Reference property is an audio clip. When this Audio Source starts playing, it will play the audio file specified in the Audio Clip attribute. An error will occur if no reference is created since there is no audio to be played. Within the Inspector, you must refer to the file. It is as simple as dragging an audio file from the Project View onto the Reference Property or using the Object Selector to do this.

References to any other type of Component, GameObject, or Asset can be included in Components. More information on assigning references may be found on the Editing Properties page.

The Audio Clip's remaining characteristics are all Value properties. These may be changed right in the Inspector. The Audio Clip's Value attributes are all toggles, numeric values, and drop-down fields, but they may also be text strings, colors, curves, and other sorts. More information on these, as well as altering value properties, may be found in the article about editing value properties.

Commands from the Component Context Menu

A component's context menu contains a number of essential commands.

The exact instructions are also accessible in the inspector through the kebab menu (three vertical dots) icon at the extreme top-right of the component's panel.

- **Reset:** This command returns the component's properties to their previous settings before the most recent editing session.
- **Remove:** If we no longer require the component associated with the GameObject, we may remove it with

the Remove Component command. It's worth noting that some component combinations rely on one another (for example, a Hinge Joint only functions if a Rigidbody is also attached); removing components that others rely on will result in a warning message.

- **Move Up/Down:** To alter the order of components of a GameObject in the Inspector, use the Move Up and Move Down commands.
- **Copy/Paste:** The Copy Component command copies a component's type and current property settings. With Paste Component Values, these may then be copied into another element of the same kind. We may also use Paste Component As New to create a new component with the copied data on an object.

Property Experimentation

While our game is in Play Mode, we may alter any GameObject's attributes in the Inspector. For example, we might wish to experiment with different leaping heights. If we add a Jump Height attribute to a script, we may test it by entering Play Mode, changing the value, and pressing the jump button to see what occurs. Then, without leaving Play Mode, we may make another modification and see the consequences in seconds. When we quit Play Mode, our properties will restore to their pre-Play Mode settings, ensuring no effort is lost. This method provides impressive flexibility to explore, tweak, and perfect your gameplay without committing to lengthy iteration cycles.

Objects That Are Primitive or Placeholders

Unity can deal with 3D models of any shape developed using modeling tools. However, various elementary object types, such as the Cube, Sphere, Capsule, Cylinder, Plane, and Quad, may be produced directly within Unity. These objects are frequently helpful in and of themselves (for example, a plane is typically used as a level ground surface), but they also provide a rapid method to generate placeholders and prototypes for testing reasons. Using the relevant item from the GameObject > 3D Object menu, any primitives can be added to the scene.

Cube

This is a basic cube with one-unit-long sides that are textured such that the picture repeats on each of the six faces. A cube isn't a particularly frequent object in most games as it is, but when scaled, it may be beneficial for walls, posts, boxes, steps, and other similar objects. It is also a helpful placeholder object for programmers to utilize during development when a completed model is unavailable. An automobile body, for example, can be crudely recreated using an extended box of nearly the proper size. Although this isn't appropriate for the entire game, it works well as a small symbolic object for testing the car's control code. Because the edges of a cube are one unit long, we may examine the proportions of a mesh imported into the scene by placing a cube nearby and comparing the sizes.

Sphere

This is a unit diameter (0.5 unit radius) sphere that has been textured such that the entire picture revolves around once, with the top and bottom "pinched" at the poles. Spheres are clearly helpful for portraying balls, planets, and missiles, but a semi-transparent sphere may also be used to show the radius of an effect in a graphical user interface (GUI).

Capsule

A capsule is a cylinder with two hemispherical covers on either end. The item has a diameter of one unit and a height of two units. It's textured such that the picture loops around precisely once, squeezed at the apex of each hemisphere. While there aren't many real-world things with this form, the capsule is a handy prototype placeholder. For specific activities, the mechanics of a rounded item are sometimes superior to those of a box.

Cylinder

This is a primary two-unit-high and one-unit-diameter cylinder that has been textured such that the image wraps once around the tube form of the body but also appears independently in the two flat, circular ends. Cylinders help make posts, rods, and wheels but keep in mind that the collider's form is a capsule (there is no primitive cylinder collider in Unity). If you require an exact cylindrical collider for physics purposes, you should generate a mesh of the proper shape in a modeling application and attach a mesh collider.

Plane

This is a flat square with ten-unit-long edges aligned in the local coordinate space's XZ plane. It's textured such that the entire image only displays once within the square. Most flat surfaces, such as floors and walls, benefit from the usage of a plane. A surface is also required for displaying pictures or videos in GUI and special effects. Although a plane may be utilized for this, the simpler quad primitive is generally a better match for the job.

Quad

The quad primitive is similar to the plane, except its edges are only one unit long, and the surface is orientated in the local coordinate space's XY plane. In addition, a quad is made up of only two triangles, whereas a plane has two hundred. A quad is proper when a scene object is only utilized as a display screen for an image or video. Quads may be used to create simple GUI and information displays and particles, sprites, and "impostor" graphics that stand in for solid objects when viewed from a distance.

Primitive 2D GameObjects

Unity includes 2D Primitive GameObjects to let us quickly prototype our Project without importing our Assets. To make 2D primitive, navigate to GameObject > 2D Object > Sprites and choose one of the following options:

- Square.
- Circle.
- Nine-Sliced.
- Isometric Diamond.
- Capsule.
- Hexagon Point-Top.
- Hexagon Flat-Top.

Sprite and Pixels-per-Unit by Default

The default Sprite size for most 2D primitives is 256 × 256 pixels, with a pixels-per-unit (PPU) size of 256, making their size equivalent to one unit in the Scene. The Capsule primitive, which is 256 × 512 pixels (1:2 units), and the Isometric Diamond primitive, which is 256 × 128 pixels, are the exceptions (1:0.5 units).

Square

The Square 2D primitive is a white square with a dimension of 1 × 1 Unity units. We may use it to build platforms rapidly or as a placeholder for other items such as barriers such as crates. We may interact with other GameObjects and 2D physics by adding the Box Collider 2D component to the GameObject. Select the Nine-Sliced option instead for a more scalable Sprite that resizes dynamically.

Circle

The Circle 2D primitive is a white circle with a diameter of one Unity unit. It may be used as a placeholder for various objects in our Scene, such as obstacles or props such as pick-ups or power-ups. We may use the Circle Collider 2D to interact with other objects and 2D physics by adding it to the GameObject.

Capsule

The Capsule 2D primitive is a white capsule with a size of 1 × 2 units. This Capsule can be used as a placeholder for many aspects of our scene, such as an obstacle, an object, or a character stand-in. We may interact with other objects and 2D physics by adding a Capsule Collider 2D to the GameObject.

Isometric Diamond

The Isometric Diamond 2D primitive is a 1 × 0.5 unit white diamond-shaped Sprite. This Sprite is intended to act as a placeholder for Isometric Tilemaps. To optimize tiling, the pixels at the top and bottom of this Sprite have been chopped significantly.

Flat-Top Hexagon

The Hexagon Flat-Top 2D primitive is a regular hexagon with sides to the top and bottom 1 unit wide. It's intended to be used as a basic Sprite placeholder for Tiles in Hexagonal Flat-Top Tilemaps. On optimize tiling, the pixels to the left and right of this Sprite have been chopped significantly.

Point-Top Hexagon

The Hexagon Point-Top 2D primitive is a one-unit-tall regular hexagon with points at the top and bottom. It's intended to be used as a basic Sprite placeholder for Tiles in Hexagonal Pointed-Top Tilemaps. To optimize tiling, the pixels at the top and bottom of this Sprite have been chopped significantly.

Nine-Sliced

The Nine-Sliced 2D primitive is a white 1 × 1 unit square with rounded corners. This Sprite has been nine-sliced, with 64-pixel boundaries on each side. It is intended for use with the Sprite Renderer's Sliced and Tiled draw modes. The nine-sliced Sprite may be used as a versatile placeholder for numerous items in our Scene and Project. To make the Sprite interact with other objects and 2D physics, add a Box Collider 2D with Auto Tiling enabled.

Scripting Is Used to Create Components

Scripting (or script creation) is the process of adding our own code modifications to the Unity Editor's capabilities utilizing the Unity Scripting API.

When we build a script and connect it to a GameObject, the script shows in the GameObject's Inspector the same way that a built-in component does. This is due to the fact that when we save a script in your project, it becomes a component.

Technically, every script we write compiles as a type of component; thus, the Unity Editor treats our script as if it were a built-in component. The Inspector exposes the elements of the script that we define, and the Editor performs any functionality we've created.

Deactivating GameObjects

To remove a GameObject from the Scene momentarily, label it as inactive. To do so, go to the Inspector and uncheck the checkbox next to the GameObject's name or use the SetActive method in the script. Check the activeSelf attribute in the script to see if an object is active or inactive.

Deactivating a Parent GameObject

When you deactivate a parent GameObject, all of its child GameObjects are likewise deactivated.

Deactivation overrides the activeSelf setting on all child GameObjects, rendering the whole hierarchy inactive from the parent down. Because this does not modify the value of the activeSelf property on the child GameObjects, they revert to their previous state when the parent is reactivated.

This implies that accessing the activeSelf property of a child GameObject will not tell you whether or not it is currently active in the Scene because even if it is set to active, one of its parents may be set to inactive.

Instead, if we need to know if it's now active in the scene, use the activeInHierarchy property, which considers its parents' overriding influence.

Tags

A Tag is a term that may be assigned to one or more GameObjects. We might, for example, create "Player" Tags for player-controlled characters and "Enemy" Tags for non-player-controlled characters. A "Collectable" Tag can be used to identify things that the player can gather in a Scene.

Tags aid in the identification of GameObjects for scripting reasons. They eliminate the need to manually add GameObjects to a script's public attributes through drag and drop, saving time when utilizing the same script code in several GameObjects.

Tags are essential in Collider control scripts for determining if the player is interacting with an opponent, a prop, or a collectible, for example.

We may find a GameObject by instructing the GameObject.FindWithTag() method to seek for any object that contains the desired Tag. GameObject is used in the following example: FindWithTag(). It creates the respawnPrefab at the position of GameObjects with the "Respawn" Tag:

```
using UnityEngine;
using System.Collections;
public class Example : MonoBehaviour
{
    public GameObject respawnPrefab;
    public GameObject respawn;
    void Start()
{
        if (respawn = = null)
            respawn = GameObject.
FindWithTag("Respawn");
        Instantiate(respawnPrefab, respawn.
transform.position, respawn.transform.
rotation) as GameObject;
    }
}
```

New Tags Creation

The Inspector displays the Tag and Layer drop-down choices directly below the name of any GameObject.

To add a new Tag, click Add Tag.... This opens the Inspector's Tag and Layer Manager. It is crucial to note that after a Tag has been named, it cannot be renamed.

Layers, like Tags, are used to specify how Unity should render GameObjects in the Scene.

Using a Tag

The Inspector displays the Tag and Layer drop-down choices directly below the name of any GameObject. To apply an existing Tag to a GameObject, enter the Tags menu and select the desired Tag. This Tag is now connected with the GameObject.

GameObjects That Remain Static

A static GameObject does not move during execution. A dynamic GameObject moves during the course of a game.

In Unity, several systems may precompute information about static GameObjects in the Editor. Because the GameObjects do not move, the results of these computations are still valid during runtime. This implies Unity can save money on runtime computations while potentially improving performance.

The Property Static Editor Flags

The Static Editor Flags property identifies the Unity systems that can use a static GameObject in their precomputations. Select which systems should include the GameObject in their precomputations using the drop-down menu. These systems have no impact when Static Editor Flags are set at runtime.

We should only include a GameObject in the precomputations if the system needs to know about it. Including a GameObject in precomputations for a system that does not need to know about that GameObject might lead to wasteful calculations, needlessly essential data files, or unexpected behavior.

The Static Editor Flags attribute is found in the Inspector for a GameObject, in the top-right corner. It consists of a checkbox that sets the value to Everything or Nothing and a drop-down menu that allows us to select which values to include.

These are the following values available:

Property:	Function:
Nothing	Do not include the GameObject in any system's precomputations.
Everything	Include the GameObject in the precomputations for all of the systems listed below.
Contribute GI	While we enable this parameter, Unity takes the target Mesh Renderer into account when calculating global illumination. These computations are done during the baking period when lighting data is being precomputed. The ContributeGI property exposes the ReceiveGI property. The ContributeGI feature has no impact unless we activate a global illumination option for the target Scene, such as Baked Global Illumination or Realtime Global Illumination. This flag is described in detail in a Unity Blog post regarding static lighting using lightprobes.
Occluder Static	In the occlusion culling system, mark the GameObject as a Static Occluder.
Occludee Static	In the occlusion culling mechanism, mark the GameObject as a Static Occludee.
Batching Static	Combine the Mesh of the GameObject with other suitable Meshes to potentially minimize runtime rendering costs.
Navigation Static	When precompiling navigation data, include the GameObject.
Off Mesh Link Generation	When precomputing navigation data, try to construct an Off-Mesh Link that begins with this GameObject.
Reflection Probe	Include this GameObject in the precomputed data for Reflection Probes with the Type attribute set to Baked.

Keeping Our Work Safe

The majority of saved data in Unity is divided into Scene modifications and Project-wide updates.

- Go to File > Save to save all Scene and Project-wide changes (or Save as). This is the quickest method for saving everything at once.
- Go to File > Save Project to save Project-wide changes but not Scene modifications.

Keep in mind that there is an exception to this rule while editing in Prefab Mode. File > Save just saves modifications to the currently open Prefab in this situation. It does not store changes to Scenes or Projects.

While we're working in the Editor, Unity automatically stores certain information.

The Scene Changes

Scene alterations involve changes to GameObjects within the Scene, such as when oneself:

- A GameObject can be added, moved, or deleted.
- In the Inspector, modify the parameters of a GameObject.

Project-Wide Modifications

Project-wide modifications in Unity affect the whole Project rather than a single Scene. Go to File > Save Project to save Project-wide settings without storing Scene modifications.

This may be beneficial if, for example, we want to build a temporary Scene to test some changes.

Among the project-wide modifications are:

When we save a project, Unity saves any changes to the Project Settings in the Library folder. The settings are saved in the following files:

```
Input: InputManager.asset
Player: ProjectSettings.asset
Tags And Layers: TagManager.asset
Time: TimeManager.asset
Physics: DynamicsManager.asset
Graphics: GraphicsSettings.asset
Physics 2D: Physics2DSettings.asset
Quality: QualitySettings.asset
Editor: EditorUserSettings.asset
Network: NetworkManager.asset
Audio: AudioManager.asset
```

- **Build Settings:** Unity stores modifications to the Build Settings as EditorBuildSettings.asset in the Library folder.
- **Modified/Changed Assets:** Unity saves any unsaved changed Assets during a save that saves Project-wide settings. This mainly pertains to Asset types that lack an Apply button in their Inspector for instant saving.
- **Dirty Assets:** Any Assets that are designated as dirty are also saved by Unity (meaning that something has touched or modified it). Custom Editors and Scripts

can be used to indicate an Asset as dirty in one of the following ways:

- Use the SerializedObject class in conjunction with SerializedProperties.
- To save changes, use the Undo class.
- If none of the other methods work, we can try SetDirty.

Immediate Saving

When certain modifications occur, Unity quickly saves them to disc. These are some examples:

- **New Assets:** Unity saves new Assets as they are created, but not future modifications to those Assets.
- **Asset Import Settings:** Most Asset kinds' Import Settings need us to hit a "Apply" button for the changes to take effect. When we click, Apply, Unity saves our modifications.
- **Baked Data:** Some sorts of data are "baked" into our Project. When each bake completes, Unity automatically stores this data. This includes the following:
  - Data on Baked Lighting.
  - Baked navigation information.
  - Data for baked occlusion culling.
- **Changes in Script Execution Order:** Unity automatically stores this information to each script's. meta file when we press the Apply button.

PREFABS

The Prefab system in Unity allows us to build, configure, and save a GameObject as a reusable Asset, replete with all of its components, property values, and child GameObjects. The Prefab Asset serves as a template for creating new Prefab instances in the Scene.

Converting a GameObject set in a certain way—such as a non-player character (NPC), prop, or piece of scenery—to a Prefab allows us to reuse it in numerous places in our Scene or across several Scenes in our Project. This is preferable to copying and pasting the GameObject since the Prefab system automatically keeps all copies in sync.

Any changes we make to a Prefab Asset are instantly mirrored in all instances of that Prefab, allowing us to make broad changes throughout our whole Project without making identical changes to each copy of the Asset.

Prefabs may be nestled inside other Prefabs to construct complicated object hierarchies that are straightforward to change at numerous levels.

This does not, however, imply that all Prefab instances must be similar. If we want certain Prefab instances to be different from others, we may override settings on specific prefab instances. We may also construct Prefab variations, which allow us to organize a collection of overrides into a meaningful version of a Prefab.

Prefabs are particularly useful when we wish to create GameObjects during runtime that did not exist in our Scene at the start, such as making powerups, special effects, projectiles, or NPCs appear at the appropriate time points throughout gameplay.

Some typical applications of prefabrication include:

- Environmental assets, such as a particular variety of tree that is utilized several times around a level.
- NPCs—for example, a specific type of robot may appear several times in our game over various levels. They can differ in their travel pace or the sound they emit (through overrides).
- Projectiles, such as a pirate's cannon, may create a cannonball Prefab each time it is fired.
- The player's primary character—the player prefab—might be put at the beginning of each level (separate Scene) of our game.

Prefabs Creation

Prefab Assets serve as templates in Unity's Prefab system. Prefab Assets are created in the Editor and stored as an asset in the Project window. Prefab Assets may be used to build an unlimited number of Prefab instances. Prefab instances may be produced in the editor and stored as part of Scenes, or they can be instantiated during runtime.

Making Prefabricated Assets

To make a Prefab Asset, drag a GameObject from the Hierarchy window into the Project window. The GameObject, along with all of its components and child GameObjects, is added to our Project window as a new Asset. Prefabs Assets are represented in the Project window by a thumbnail depiction of the GameObject or the blue cube Prefab icon, based on how our Project window is set up.

The original GameObject is also converted into a Prefab instance during the Prefab Asset creation process. It is now a child of the newly formed Prefab Asset. Prefab instances are displayed in blue text in the Hierarchy, and the root GameObject of the Prefab is indicated with the blue cube Prefab icon rather than the red, green, and blue GameObject icons.

Prefab Instance Creation

We may construct instances of the Prefab Asset in the Editor by dragging it from the Project view to the Hierarchy view.

Scripting may also be used to construct Prefab objects at runtime.

Replacement of Existing Prefabs

We may change a Prefab asset in the Project window by dragging a new GameObject from the Hierarchy window and putting it on top of an existing Prefab object.

When we replace an existing Prefab, Unity strives to keep references to the Prefab and its constituent pieces, such as child GameObjects and Components, intact. This is accomplished by matching the names of GameObjects between the new Prefab and the current Prefab that is being replaced.

Because this matching is done by only name, it is difficult to predict which GameObject will be matched if the Prefab's hierarchy contains several GameObjects with the same name.

As a result, if we want to save our references while saving over an existing prefab, we must give each GameObject in the Prefab a unique name.

Also, if a single GameObject within the Prefab has more than one of the same Component type connected, we may have a similar difficulty when saving over an existing Prefab to retain references to existing Components. It is impossible to foresee which of them will be matched to the current references in this scenario.

Prefab Editing in Prefab Mode

Open a Prefab Asset in Prefab Mode to alter it. Prefab Mode lets us examine and modify the Prefab Asset's contents independently of any other GameObjects in our Scene. Changes made in Prefab Mode have an effect on all instances of that Prefab.

Prefab Mode Entry and Exit

A Prefab Asset can be edited in isolation or in context.

- When we edit a Prefab in isolation, Unity conceals the rest of our current working Scene and only shows us the GameObjects that are related to the Prefab.
- When we modify a Prefab in context, the remainder of our current working Scene stays visible but not editable.

Isolation Editing

In Prefab Mode, we may start editing a Prefab in a variety of ways. We may open a Prefab Asset and change it separately in the following ways:

- In the Project window, double-click the Prefab Asset.
- In the Project window, choose a Prefab Asset and then click the Open Prefab button in the Inspector window.

When we enter Prefab Mode by itself, Unity displays only the contents of that Prefab in the Scene view and the Hierarchy pane. The root of the Prefab is a standard GameObject; it lacks the blue Prefab instance indicator.

The Scene view in Prefab Mode has a breadcrumb bar at the top. The Prefab that is now open is the one on the right. To return to the main Scenes or other Prefab Assets that we may have opened, use the breadcrumb bar.

At the top of the Hierarchy window, there is a Prefab header bar that displays the currently active Prefab. We may move back one step by clicking the back arrow in the header bar, identical to clicking the breadcrumb in the breadcrumb bar in the Scene view.

Contextual Editing

We may also open a Prefab Asset in Context by using an instance of that Prefab. There are several ways to accomplish this, including:

In the Inspector window, choose a Prefab instance from the Hierarchy pane and click the Open button.

In the Hierarchy pane, choose a Prefab instance and hit P on the keyboard. This is the standard keyboard binding.

In the Hierarchy pane, click the arrow button next to the Prefab instance.

Unity shows the visual representation of the context in grey scale by default to visually separate it from the Prefab contents you change. However, we can utilize the Prefab bar's Context: control to change it to any of the following states:

- **Normal:** Displays the context in its default colors.
- **Grayscale:** Displays the context in grayscale.
- **Hidden:** Hides the context thoroughly, revealing only the Prefab content.

The GameObjects that are part of the context cannot be selected, nor do they appear in the Hierarchy. This allows us to focus on developing our Prefab without unintentionally choosing unrelated GameObjects or having a messy Hierarchy pane. When we move GameObjects that are part of the Prefab contents, we may utilize Unity's snapping functionality to snap to GameObjects in the context, as long as the context is not set to Hidden.

In Prefab Mode in Context, Unity shows the Prefab contents in the same place as the Prefab instance from which it was accessed. This implies that we may see a preview of the Prefab contents' base transform with different position and rotation values than the Prefab Asset possesses.

These settings are not editable in Context's Prefab Mode. If we need to make changes, we may either open the Prefab in isolation or select the Prefab Asset in the Project window and make changes in the Inspector.

Aside from the root Transform attributes, we may also override additional characteristics of a Prefab instance, which may radically alter its look compared to the Prefab Asset of which it is an instance. To see these overridden values from the Prefab instance, activate the Show Overrides checkbox in the Prefab bar when in Prefab Mode in Context. Any properties that we override on the Prefab instance are previewed the same way on the Prefab contexts while this option is active, and we cannot alter them. Disable the Show Overrides option once again to change those properties.

Save Automatically

In the upper right corner of the Scene view, an Auto Save is setting for Prefab Mode. When we activate it, Unity stores any changes we make to a Prefab to the Prefab Asset. By default, Auto Save is enabled.

Disable the Auto Save option if we want to make changes without immediately storing them in the Preset Asset. When we exit Prefab Mode for the current Prefab, Unity asks if we will save unsaved modifications. Turning off Auto Save may assist if editing a Prefab in Prefab Mode appears sluggish.

Changing from Isolation to Context Mode

When we launch Prefab Mode from a Prefab Asset, Unity isolates the Prefab's contents. When we activate Prefab Mode through a Prefab instance in the Hierarchy window, Prefab Mode in Context is launched.

When we launch Prefab Mode in this manner, the context of the Prefab instance is visible in the Scene view, even though you are not changing the instance but rather the Prefab Asset itself. For example, if we activate Prefab Mode in Context through a Prefab instance in a Scene, we may see the Scene's surroundings while editing the Prefab. The lighting conditions in the Prefab are also the same as in the Scene.

If we wish to access a Prefab instance in isolation rather than context, hold down the Alt key and click the Activate button or the arrow button to open Prefab Mode. We can also create a custom shortcut in the Shortcuts box using the command Stage > Edit Prefab in Isolation.

Undo

When we make changes to a Prefab Asset while it is in Prefab Mode, you can only undo those changes while it is still in Prefab Mode. When we quit Prefab Mode for a specific Prefab Asset, our modifications for that Prefab Asset are no longer visible in the undo history.

Environment for Editing

In Isolation, we may utilize a Scene as an editing environment for Prefab Mode. This allows us to change your Prefab against a custom backdrop rather than an empty Scene. This might be beneficial if we want to examine how our Prefab looks against a specific backdrop of our choosing. When you enter Prefab Mode in Isolation, Unity only utilizes this editing environment.

In Prefab Mode, you cannot pick the GameObjects in the Scene that we have assigned as the editing environment, nor do they appear in the Hierarchy. This allows us to focus on developing our Prefab without unintentionally choosing unrelated GameObjects or having a messy Hierarchy pane.

Open the Editor window (top menu: Edit > Project Settings, then choose the Editor category) and navigate to the Prefab Editing Environment section to designate a Scene as the editing environment.

For "non-UI" Prefabs, use the Regular Environment setting, while for UI Prefabs, use the UI Environment setting. UI Prefabs have a Rect Transform component on the root instead of a standard Transform component. Prefabs with a regular Transform component are considered "non-UI."

Overrides for Instances

Instance overrides enable us to define differences amongst Prefab instances while still connecting them to the same Prefab Asset.

When we make modifications to a Prefab Asset, they are mirrored in all of its instances. However, we may also make changes to a specific instance. This establishes an instance override in that particular instance.

For example, suppose we had a Prefab Asset called "Robot" that we used in many levels of our game. Each "Robot" instance, on the other hand, has a different speed value and an allocated audio clip.

Instance overrides are classified into four types:

1. Overriding a property's value.

2. Including a new component.

3. Taking out a component.

4. Creating a new child GameObject.

Prefab instances have several limitations: you cannot reparent a GameObject that is part of a Prefab, and you cannot delete a GameObject that is part of the Prefab. However, we may deactivate a GameObject, which is an acceptable option for uninstalling a GameObject (this counts as a property override).

In the Inspector window, instance overrides are highlighted with a bold name label and a blue line in the left margin. The blue line in the margin covers the whole component when we add a new element to a Prefab instance.

Added and deleted components have plus and minus badges on their Inspector icons, while added GameObjects have a plus badge on their Hierarchy icon.

Overrides Are Given Precedence

A Prefab instance's overridden property value always takes priority over the value from the Prefab Asset. This implies that changing a Prefab Asset's property does not affect instances when that property is overridden.

Whether we make a modification to a Prefab Asset and it does not update all instances as intended, we should check to see if that property on the instance is overridden. It is advisable to utilize instance overrides only when required. If our Project has a significant number of instance overrides, it might be challenging to know whether our modifications to the Prefab Asset will or will not affect all instances.

The Alignment Is Unique to the Prefab Instance

A Prefab instance's alignment is a specific circumstance that is treated differently than other attributes. Alignment values are never sent from the Prefab Asset to the Prefab instances. This implies they can always deviate from the alignment of the Prefab Asset without requiring an explicit instance override. In particular, the alignment refers to the Position and Rotation properties of the Prefab instance's root Transform, and for a Rect Transform, this also includes the Width, Height, Margins, Anchors, and Pivot values.

This is due to the rarity of requiring numerous copies of a Prefab to adopt the same position and rotation. Most of the time, you'll want our prefab instances to be in various locations and rotations, so Unity doesn't consider these to be Prefab overrides.

Changing a Prefab's Occurrences

The Inspector for a Prefab instance's root contains three extra controls than a standard GameObject: Open, Select, and Overrides.

The Open button in Prefab Mode opens the Prefab Asset from which the instance is derived, allowing us to edit the Prefab Asset and thereby change all of its instances. The Select button in the Project window picks the Prefab Asset from which this instance is created. The Overrides button activates the Overrides drop-down menu.

Dropdown Overrides

The Customizations drop-down pane displays all of the Prefab instance's overrides. It also allows us to add instance overrides to the Prefab Asset or revert instance overrides to the Prefab Asset's values. The Overrides drop-down button shows only for the root Prefab instance, not for Prefabs inside Prefabs.

The Overrides drop-down box allows us to apply or revert individual prefab overrides or to apply or revert all prefab overrides at once.

- The Prefab Asset is altered when an override is applied. This adds the override (which is presently only available on our Prefab instance) to the Asset. This indicates that the Prefab Asset now has that alteration, and the Prefab instance no longer contains it as an override.
- The Prefab instance is altered when an override is reverted. This effectively discards our override and returns the Prefab Asset to its original state.

The drop-down pane displays a list of modifications made to the instance, such as changed, added, and removed components and new GameObjects.

To view an entry, click on it. This opens a floating window that displays the modification and allows you to reverse or apply it.

The view compares the component's values on the Prefab Asset with the changed component on the Prefab instance for components with modified values. This enables us to compare the original Prefab Asset values to the current overrides and determine whether to rollback or apply those values.

The "GermOBlaster" child GameObject in the example exists on both the Prefab Asset and the Prefab instance, but its scale has been raised on the instance. This increase in scale is an instance override, and it can be viewed in the Overrides drop-down pane as a side-by-side comparison.

Revert All and Apply All options are now available in the Overrides drop-down menu for reversing or applying all modifications at once. If we have Prefabs within Prefabs, the Apply All button always applies to the outermost Prefab, which has the Overrides drop-down button on its root GameObject.

When we choose several items at the same time, the Revert All and Apply All buttons are replaced by Revert Selected and Apply Selected buttons. These can be used to rollback or apply numerous overrides at the same time. The Apply Selected button, like the Apply All button, always applies to the outermost Prefab.

Menus in Context

Instead of utilizing the Overrides drop-down window, you may rollback and apply specific overrides using the Inspector's context menu.

Overridden attributes are shown in bold. They can be undone or applied via a context menu:

Modified components can be reversed or applied using the component header's cog drop-down button or context menu:

Components that have been added have a plus badge that appears above the icon. They may be reversed or applied using the component header's cog drop-down button.

Components that have been removed have a minus badge that appears over the icon. The removal can be reversed or applied using the component header's cog drop-down button or context menu. Reverting the removal restores the component, whereas performing the removal deletes it from the Prefab Asset.

When a GameObject (including other Prefabs) is added as a child to a Prefab instance, a plus badge appears above the icon in the Hierarchy. They may be reversed or applied through the context menu on the Hierarchy object.

Prefabs That Are Nested

Prefab instances can be included within other Prefabs. This is known as nested Prefabs. Nested Prefabs keep ties to their respective Prefab Assets while simultaneously being a component of another Prefab Asset.

In Prefab Mode, Add a Nested Prefab

In Prefab Mode, we may add and operate with Prefab instances in the same way we would in Scenes. We may move a Prefab Asset from the Project window to the

Hierarchy window or Scene view by dragging it from the Project window to make a Prefab instance from that Asset within the Prefab you're working on.

Take note of the root GameObject the blue cube Prefab icon is not displayed for the Prefab that is open in Prefab Mode, but it is displayed for any instances of other Prefabs. Like with Prefab instances in scenes, we can also apply overrides to these Prefab instances.

Prefabs Can Be Nested Using Their Instances

We may also add a Prefab instance as a child to another Prefab instance in the Scene without entering Prefab Mode, just like any other GameObject. In the Hierarchy, such an extra Prefab instance has a plus badge overlaid on the icon, indicating that it is an override on that specific instance of the outer Prefab.

The additional Prefab can be reversed or applied to the outer Prefab in the same manner as other overrides (through the Overrides drop-down window or the context menu on the GameObject in the Hierarchy) detailed in Editing a Prefab via its instances. Only the outer Prefab has the Overrides drop-down button. Once applied, the Prefab no longer displays the plus badge since it is no longer an override but is instead nested within the outer Prefab Asset itself. It keeps its blue cube symbol because it is a Prefab instance in its own right, and it keeps its link to its Prefab Asset.

Prefabs That Are Nested

Prefab instances can be included within other Prefabs. This is known as nested Prefabs. Nested Prefabs keep ties to their respective Prefab Assets while simultaneously being a component of another Prefab Asset.

In Prefab Mode, Add a Nested Prefab

In Prefab Mode, we may add and operate with Prefab instances in the same way we would in Scenes. Drag a Prefab Asset from the Project window to the Hierarchy window or Scene view to create a Prefab instance from that Asset within the open Prefab.

Note that the blue cube Prefab icon does not appear on the root GameObject of a Prefab that is open in Prefab Mode, but it does appear on any instances of other Prefabs. Like with Prefab instances in scenes, we can also apply overrides to these Prefab instances.

Prefabs Can Be Nested Using Their Instances

We may also add a Prefab instance as a child to another Prefab instance in the Scene without entering Prefab Mode, just like any other GameObject. In the Hierarchy, such an extra Prefab instance has a plus badge overlaid on the icon, indicating that it is an override on that specific instance of the outer Prefab.

The additional Prefab can be reversed or applied to the outer Prefab in the same manner as other overrides (through the Overrides drop-down window or the context menu on the GameObject in the Hierarchy) detailed in Editing a Prefab via its instances. Only the outer Prefab has the Overrides drop-down button. Once applied, the Prefab no longer displays the plus badge since it is no longer an override but is instead nested within the outer Prefab Asset itself. It keeps its blue cube symbol because it is a Prefab instance in its own right, and it keeps its link to its Prefab Asset.

Prefab Variations

Prefab Variants come in handy when we need a collection of predefined versions of a Prefab.

For example, we could wish to include a variety of GermSlimeTargets in our game, all of which are built on the same core GermSlimeTarget Prefab. However, we may want some GermSlimeTargets to carry objects, travel at various speeds, or produce additional sound effects.

To do this, we might configure our first GermSlimeTarget Prefab to execute all of the core activities that all GermSlimeTarget should share and then construct numerous Prefab Variants to:

- Use a property override on a script to adjust the pace of a GermSlimeTarget.
- Attach an extra GameObject to a GermSlimeTarget's arm to have it hold an object.
- Add an AudioSource component that plays a squelching sound to GermSlimeTarget to give it a slug-like squelch.

A Prefab Variant inherits the attributes of another Prefab, which is referred to as the base. Overrides applied to the Prefab Variant take precedence over the settings of the basic Prefab. A Prefab Variant can be based on any other Prefab, including Model Prefabs and different Prefab Variants.

Developing a Prefab Variant

There are several methods for creating a Prefab Variant based on another Prefab.

In the Project view, right-click on a Prefab and choose to Create > Prefab Variant. This generates a variation of the specified Prefab with no overrides at first. To begin adding overrides to the Prefab Variant, open it in Prefab Mode.

In addition, we may drag a Prefab instance from the Hierarchy into the Project window. When we do this, a dialogue box appears asking us whether we want to create a new Original Prefab or a Prefab Variant.

When we select Prefab Variant, a new Prefab Variant is created based on the Prefab instance that dragged. Any customizations we had on that instance have now been included in the new Prefab Variant. We may open it in Prefab Mode to add more overrides and change or remove existing ones.

Prefab Variants that have the blue Prefab icon with arrows.

Prefab Variant Editing

When we open a Prefab Variant in Prefab Mode, the root is displayed as a Prefab instance with the blue Prefab icon. This Prefab instance represents the basic Prefab from which the Prefab Variant derives, not the Prefab Variant itself. Any changes we make to the Prefab Variant become overrides to the Variant's base.

Because the Prefab instance is an instance of the base Prefab GermSlimeTarget and the Select button always selects the Prefab Asset from which an example is created, if we choose the GermSlimeTarget With GermOBlaster root GameObject and then click the Select button in the Inspector, it will select the base Prefab GermSlimeTarget rather than the Variant GermSlimeTarget With GermOBlaster.

Prefab overrides, such as updated property values, new components, deleted components, and additional child GameObjects, may be used in a Prefab Variant just like any other Prefab instance. There are also the same restrictions: we cannot reparent GameObjects in the Prefab Variant derived from its original Prefab. We can't also remove a GameObject from a Prefab Variant if it's still in its base Prefab. However, we may deactivate GameObjects (through a property override) to have the same result as uninstalling a GameObject.

When updating a Prefab Variant in Prefab Mode, consider that applying these overrides (through the Overrides drop-down window or context menus) will result in our variant's variants being applied to the underlying Prefab Asset. This is frequently not what we desire. The purpose of a Prefab Variant is to give a handy method to store a valuable and reusable collection of overrides; therefore, they should generally remain as overrides and not be applied to the underlying Prefab Asset. To demonstrate, if we added the GermOBlaster GameObject to the basic Prefab Asset (the "GermSlimeTarget"), the Prefab Asset would also include the GermOBlaster.

The whole idea of the GermSlimeTarget With GermOBlaster version is that it is the only one with a GermOBlaster; hence, the additional GermOBlaster GameObject should be left as an override inside the Prefab Variant.

When we open the Overrides drop-down window, we can always see in the header which object the overrides are for and which context the overrides reside in. The header for a Prefab Variant will state that the overrides are to the basic Prefab and reside in the Prefab Variant. To be sure, the Apply All button also states Apply All to Base.

Multiple Layers of Override

Overrides can exist at numerous levels when working with Prefabs inside other Prefabs or with Prefab Variants, and the same overrides can be applied to multiple distinct Prefabs.

Apply Target Selection

When we have a Prefab instance with nested Prefabs or a Prefab Variant, we may be able to choose which Prefab an override should be applied to.

Consider a Prefab "Vase" that is nested within a Prefab "Table," and the scene has a "Table" Prefab instance.

If a property on "Vase" is overridden in this case, the override might be applied to either the "Vase" or the "Table."

The Apply, All button in the Overrides drop-down menu only allows us to apply the override to the outer Prefab—in this example, the "Table." However, when applying using the context menu or the comparative view for individual components in the Overrides drop-down window, we may select an apply target.

If we pick Apply to Prefab "Vase" in this example, the value is applied to the "Vase" Prefab Asset and is utilized for all instances of the "Vase" Prefab.

Furthermore, if we select Apply as Override in Prefab "Table," the value becomes an override on the example of "Vase" contained within the "Table" Prefab. The property on the instance in the Scene is no longer tagged as an override, but if we open the "Table" Prefab in Prefab Mode, the property on the "Vase" Prefab example is marked as an override.

When overriding as an override in the "Table" Prefab Asset, the "Vase" Prefab Asset is unaffected. This implies that all instances of the "Table" Prefab have the updated value on their "Vase" Prefab instance, but other instances of the "Vase" Prefab are not part of the "Table" Prefab are unaffected.

If the property on the "Vase" Prefab is updated later, it will affect all instances of the "Vase" Prefab unless that property is overridden. Because it is overridden on the "Vase" instance within the "Table" Prefab, the modification will not affect any of the "Vase" instances that are part of "Table" instances.

Applying to inner prefabs may have an impact on outside prefabs as well.

When one or more properties are applied to an inner Prefab Asset, its overrides are reverted in the outer Prefabs, occasionally resulting in changes to outer Prefab Assets.

In our example, if Apply to Prefab "Vase" is selected and the "Table" Prefab contains an override of the value, the override in the "Table" Prefab is reverted and property simultaneously on the instance preserves the value that was just applied. If this were not the case, the value of the example would change immediately after it was applied.

Prefab Instance Unpacking

Unpacking a Prefab instance returns the contents of the Prefab instance to a standard GameObject. This is the exact opposite of generating (packing) a Prefab, except that it does not delete the Prefab Asset and just impacts the Prefab instance.

Unpacking a Prefab instance is as simple as right-clicking on it in the Hierarchy and selecting Unpack Prefab. The generated GameObject in the Scene is no longer linked to its previous Prefab Asset. This procedure does not affect the Prefab Asset itself, and there may still be instances of it in our Project.

If we override your Prefab instance before unpacking it, they will be "baked" onto the resultant GameObjects. That is, the values will remain unchanged, but they will no longer have the status as overrides since there is no Prefab to override.

When we unpack a Prefab containing nested Prefabs, the nested Prefabs continue to be Prefab instances with connections to their respective Prefab Assets. Similarly, when we unpack a Prefab Variant, a new Prefab instance is created at the root that is an instance of the basic Prefab.

In general, unpacking a Prefab instance returns the same items that we see when we enter Prefab Mode for that Prefab. This is due to the fact that Prefab Mode displays the contents of a Prefab, and unpacking a Prefab instance unpacks the contents of a Prefab.

If we wish to replace a Prefab instance with normal GameObjects and delete any ties to any Prefab Assets, right-click on it in the Hierarchy and select Unpack Prefab Completely. This is identical to unpacking the Prefab and continuing to unpack any Prefab instances that occur due to being nested or base Prefabs.

Prefab instances that reside in Scenes or inside other Prefabs can be unpacked.

Unity3D Fundamentals—A Quick Look at Game Physics

Unity is an undeniably powerful game engine. As a result, it develops its method for modeling physics in a highly efficient manner. Unity defines it as:

To identify interactions between GameObjects, Unity uses Rigidbodies and Colliders. It should be remembered that Unity contains two distinct systems that cannot communicate with one another: a 3D Physics system and a 2D Physics system.

- **In a Nutshell:**
    - **Rigidbody Element:** This component is in charge of applying physics simulations to GameObjects such as Gravity and attributes such as Mass and Velocity. It is a necessary component in identifying collisions. In Unity, there are two sorts of Rigidbody Components: 3D and 2D. It is critical to choose the appropriate one for the kind of setting in which you operate.
    - **Collider Component:** Consider this component to be the volume of space that our item occupies. Colliders provide a method for registering collisions between objects in the scene. They come in a variety of forms and sizes to suit our needs. The Collider, like the Rigidbody, must be chosen correctly for Unity to detect collisions accurately. If we're working in 3D, ensure sure our GameObjects aren't accidentally utilizing 2D Colliders. Fortunately, all Colliders are labeled explicitly.

Let's take a brief look at an example of elementary physics applied to a GameObject. We will make a cube to serve as our floor and a spherical to act as a ball for physics simulations:

Colliders are linked to both the floor and the ball. The Sphere Collider tied to our ball may be seen in the inspector, but nothing happens when pressing the Play button. Unity has no means of knowing what that GameObject should do.

Let's give the sphere a Rigidbody. It is not essential to add one to the floor because the sphere will handle all collision occurrences in this case:

We chose "RigidBody" rather than "RigidBody2D" because this is a 3D project using 3D Colliders.

Now, let's press the Play button:

Our ball is now impacted by the Rigidbody's Gravity and proceeds to fall until it finds a contact. This example collides with the floor and is halted by the Box Collider tied to it. The inspector displays the numbers for the ball's Speed, Velocity, and World Center of Mass as they change during its descent.

Only the ball has a Rigidbody Component linked to it, and it can detect the collider on the floor and simulate their contact.

Physics

Unity allows us to simulate physics in our project to verify that objects accelerate and behave appropriately to collisions, gravity, and other forces. Unity has many physics engine implementations that we may utilize depending on the demands of our project: 3D, 2D, object-oriented, or data-oriented.

Object-Oriented Projects with Built-In Physics Engines

If our project is object-oriented, utilize the physics engine integrated with Unity that best suits our needs:

- 3D physics built-in.
- There is built-in 2D physics.

For Object-Oriented Tasks, Use 3D Physics

This section outlines the primary components accessible via Unity's built-in 3D physics engine, which may be used to object-oriented programs. It contains the following items:

- A summary of the major physics concepts: Rigidbodies, Collisions, and Joints Character Controllers, physics articulations, and physics articulations.
- Some examples of explanations for certain physics contexts: Continuous collision detection as well as multi-scene physics.
- The Physics Debug Visualization is described in detail.

Furthermore, the 3D Physics Reference part includes a full description of all accessible components, and the Physics HOWTOs section includes a few pointers on typical physics-related activities.

2D Physics Reference

Use the above attributes as global settings for Physics 2D. If we wish to manage the global 3D physics parameters, use the Physics Manager settings instead.

The Physics 2D parameters define the physics simulation's precision. More processing overhead is required for a more realistic simulation, and these options allow us to modify the trade-off between accuracy and performance that is best suited to our project.

CHAPTER 4

Animation in Unity

Retargetable animations, complete control over animation weights at runtime, event calling from within the animation playback, advanced state machine hierarchies and transitions, blend shapes for face animations, and many more capabilities are available in Unity Animation. Let us take a closer look at animations in Unity.

OVERVIEW OF THE ANIMATION SYSTEM

Unity features a complex and powerful animation system (known as "Mecanim"). It includes:

- Simple workflow and animation setup for all Unity elements, including objects, characters, and attributes.
- Humanoid animation retargeting the ability to apply animations from one character model to another. Support for imported animation clips and animation developed within Unity.

DOI: 10.1201/9781003214755-4

- Workflow for aligning animation clips has been simplified.
- Convenient previewing of animation clips, transitions, and interactions. This enables animators to work independently of programmers, prototyping and previewing their animations before the gameplay code is hooked in.
- A visual programming tool is used to manage intricate relationships between animations.
- Animating various body sections using different reasoning.
- Layering and masking are valuable features.

WORKFLOW FOR ANIMATION

The animation system in Unity is built on the notion of Animation Clips, which hold information about how specific objects' position, rotation, or other attributes should change over time. Each clip can be considered a single linear recording. External animation clips are made by artists or animators using third-party technologies such as Autodesk® 3ds Max® or Autodesk® Maya®, or they originate from motion capture studios or other sources.

The animation clips are then organized into a flowchart-like system known as an Animator Controller.

The Animator Controller functions as a "State Machine," keeping track of which clip should be played at any given time and when the animations should change or blend.

A straightforward Animator Controller could comprise one or two clips, for example, to manage the spinning and bouncing of a powerup or to animate a door opening and closing at the appropriate moment. A more powerful Animator Controller may have hundreds of humanoid animations for all of the main character's motions and the ability to mix between numerous clips at once to give a smooth motion as the player walks across the area.

Unity's Animation system also includes several unique features for working with humanoid characters, such as the ability to retarget humanoid animation from any source (for example, motion capture, the Asset Store, or another third-party animation library) to our character model, as well as adjust muscle definitions. Unity's Avatar system, which maps humanoid avatars to a standard internal structure, enables several particular functionalities.

The Animator Component connects each of these parts—the Animation Clips, the Animator Controller, and the Avatar—to a GameObject. This component contains a reference to an Animator Controller and (if applicable) the Avatar for this model. The Animator Controller, in turn, stores references to the Animation Clips that it employs.

- The animation clips are either imported from another source or generated within Unity.
- An Animator Controller is where the animation clips are inserted and organized. In the Animator window,

this is a view of an Animator Controller. States (which can represent animations or nested sub-state machines) are defined as nodes connected by lines. This Animator Controller may be found in the Project window as an Asset.

- The rigged character model has a unique bone structure that is transferred to Unity's standard Avatar format. This mapping is saved as an Avatar Asset as part of the imported character model, and it is also visible in the Project window.
- When animating the character model, an Animator component is linked to it. The Animator Component, which has both the Animator Controller and the Avatar assigned, may be seen in the Inspector view. The animator combines these to animate the model. When animating a humanoid figure, the Avatar reference is only essential. Only an Animator Controller is required for other sorts of animation.

SYSTEM OF LEGACY ANIMATION

While Mecanim is preferred in most cases, Unity has kept its heritage animation technology before Unity 4. When working with older content generated before Unity 4, we may need to utilize it.

Clips of Animation

Animation Clips are a key component of Unity's animation system. Unity allows for the import of animation from other sources and creating animation clips from scratch within the editor through the Animation window.

Externally Sourced Animation

Externally imported animation clips might include:

- Humanoid animations shot at a motion capture studio.
- An artist creates animations from scratch in an external three-dimensional (3D) application (such as Autodesk® 3ds Max® or Autodesk® Maya®).
- Third-party library animation sets (for example, from Unity's Asset shop).
- A single imported timeline was used to trim and slice several clips.

Unity Was Used to Create and Edit the Animation

We may also generate and edit animation clips in Unity's Animation Window. These clips are capable of animating:

- GameObjects' location, rotation, and scale.
- Component attributes include material color, light intensity, and the sound loudness.
- We may use float, integer, enum, vector, and Boolean variables in our scripts.
- The order in which functions are called within our scripts.

EXTERNALLY SOURCED ANIMATION

External animation is imported into Unity in the same manner that standard 3D files are. These files can contain animation data in the form of a linear recording of the motions of objects inside the file, whether they are Generic FBX files or native formats from 3D applications such as Autodesk® Maya®, Cinema 4D, Autodesk® 3ds Max®, or BlenderTM.

In some cases, the item to be animated (for example, a character) and the animations associated with it can be found in the same file. In other circumstances, the animations may be stored in a different file from the object being animated.

It's possible that animations are model-specific and cannot be reused on other models. A big octopus end-boss in your game, for example, may have a unique arrangement of limbs and bones, as well as its own set of motions.

In other cases, we may have a library of animations that we want to utilize on different models in our scenario. For example, several humanoid figures may all utilize the same walk and run animations. In these cases, it's typical to include a small placeholder model in our animation files for previewing. Alternatively, animation files can be used even if they contain no geometry and only the animation data.

When importing several animations, they can reside as different files within our project folder, or we can extract numerous animation clips from a single FBX file if produced as takes from Motion Builder or with a plugin/script for Autodesk® Maya®, Autodesk® 3ds Max®, or other 3D products. If our file has numerous different animations grouped on a single timeline, we may wish to do this. A long motion-recorded timeline, for example, may have the animation for a few distinct jump motions, and we may want to trim out specific bits of this to utilize as individual clips and delete the rest. When we load all animations into one timeline, Unity includes animation cutting tools that allow us to set the frame range for each clip.

Importing Animation Files

Any animation must be imported into our project before it can be utilized in Unity. Unity supports native Autodesk® Maya® (.mb or.ma), Autodesk® 3ds Max® (.max), and BlenderTM (.blend) files, as well as Generic FBX files generated from most animation packages. It should be noted that importing from .blend files necessitates the installation of BlenderTM locally.

Data from Imported Animation Files May Be Seen and Copied

In the Animation pane, we can see the keyframes and curves of imported animation clips. When these imported clips include a lot of bones and keyframes, the amount of information might appear overwhelming.

Select the individual bones we want to look at to narrow down the view. The keyframes or curves for those bones are then displayed in the Animation window.

When examining imported Animation keyframes, the Animation window displays the Animation data in a read-only mode.

To modify this data, open Unity and create a new empty Animation Clip (see Creating a New Animation Clip), then select, copy, and paste the Animation data from the imported Animation Clip into your new, editable Animation Clip.

AVATARS WITH HUMANOID

The Unity Animation System includes features designed specifically for working with humanoid characters. Because humanoid figures are ubiquitous in games, Unity consists of a specific workflow and a comprehensive toolset for humanoid animations.

Unity's Avatar system determines if an animated model is humanoid in layout and which model portions correlate to the legs, arms, head, and body.

Because the bone structures of numerous humanoid figures are identical, it is possible to transfer motions from one to the other, permitting retargeting and inverse kinematics__ (IK)__.

ADDING HUMANOID MOVEMENTS TO A MODEL

This webinar will guide us through the steps of importing a model for use with Unity's Animation System.

The Animation System supports two kinds of models:

1. A humanoid model is a specialized structure containing at least 15 bones that are structured to adhere to a real human skeleton loosely. This page offers information on how to import this type of model.

2. Everything else is a Generic model. This might range from a teakettle to a dragon. See Importing a model with non-humanoid animations for details on how to do so.

Overview

When Unity imports Model files containing Humanoid Rigs and Animation, it must reconcile the Model's bone structure to its Animation. It accomplishes this by mapping each bone in the file to a Humanoid Avatar so that the Animation may be correctly played. Because of all this, it is critical to prepare our Model file before importing it into Unity thoroughly.

- Create the Avatar and define the Rig type.
- Correct or confirm the mapping of the Avatar.
- When we're done with the bone mapping, we may go to the Muscles & Settings tab to change the Avatar's muscle configuration.
- We may save the mapping of your skeleton's bones to the Avatar as a Human Template (.ht) file if you like.
- By designing an Avatar Mask, we may limit the animation that is imported on certain bones.
- Enable the Import Animation option from the Animation tab before configuring the other Asset-specific settings.
- If the file has numerous animations or actions, you may use Animation Clips to specify particular action ranges.
    - Alter the posture and root transformation.
    - Looping should be optimized.
    - The animation should be replicated on both sides of the humanoid skeleton.
    - To animate the timings of other things, add curves to the clip.
    - Add events to the clip to activate specific actions in sync with the animation.

    - Discard a portion of the animation the same way as a runtime Avatar Mask would, but this time at import time.
    - To drive the action, select a different Root Motion Node.
    - Read any messages from Unity regarding the import of the clip.
    - View a sneak peek of the animation clip.
- To save our changes, select the Apply button at the bottom of the Import Settings window, or Revert to reverse them.

Avatar Setup

Set the Animation Type to Humanoid on the Inspector window's Rig tab. The Avatar Definition attribute is set to Create from This Model by default. If we preserve this option, Unity will attempt to map the set of bones described in the file to a Humanoid Avatar.

In certain circumstances, we may alter this option to Copy From Other Avatar to utilize an Avatar we've already created for another Model file. For example, suppose we construct a Mesh (skin) in our 3D modeling application with multiple individual animations. In that case, you may export the Mesh to a single FBX file and each animation to a separate FBX file. When importing these files into Unity, we need to make one Avatar for the first file (usually the Mesh). We may reuse that Avatar for the rest of the files as long as they all utilize the same bone structure (for example, all the animations).

If we activate this option, we must set the Source attribute to designate the Avatar we wish to use.

We can also change the maximum number of bones that can affect a single vertex with the Skin Weights property. This parameter restricts impact to four bones by default, but we can select more or less.

Unity attempts to match the current bone structure to the Avatar bone structure when clicking the Apply button. It can accomplish this automatically in many circumstances by examining the relationships between the bones in the rig.

A check mark displays next to the Configure menu if the match is successful. In addition, Unity adds an Avatar sub-Asset to the Model Asset, which can be found in the Project view.

Unity was able to match the essential bones, resulting in a successful match. However, for best results, match the optional bones and place the model in a suitable T-pose.

If Unity is unable to build the Avatar, across shows next to the Configure button, and there is no Avatar sub-Asset in the Project view.

Because the Avatar is such a crucial part of the animation system, we must configure it correctly for our Model.

As a result, regardless of whether the automated Avatar creation succeeds or fails, we should constantly double-check that our Avatar is legitimate and correctly set up.

Configure the Avatar

If we wish to verify that Unity correctly mapped your model's bones to the Avatar, or if Unity failed to construct the Avatar for your model, we may enter the Avatar configuration mode by clicking the Configure… button on the Rig tab.

If Unity produces an Avatar successfully, the Avatar appears as a sub-Asset of the model Asset. Pick the Avatar Asset in the Project window and click the "Configure Avatar" button in the Inspector to enter the Avatar configuration mode. This mode enables us to see and modify how Unity maps your model's bones to the Avatar layout.

When we enter Avatar configuration mode, the Avatar window in the Inspector displays, displaying bone mapping.

Check that the bone mapping is proper and that Unity did not assign any optional bones to be mapped.

For Unity to create a valid match, our skeleton must have at least the required bones in place. To increase our chances of discovering a match for the Avatar, name our bones after the body parts they represent. For example, the terms "LeftArm" and "RightForearm" make it obvious what these bones regulate.

Strategy Mapping

If the model does not produce a proper match, we can use a similar procedure to the one Unity employs:

- To clear any mapping that Unity tried, select Clear from the Mapping option at the bottom of the Avatar window.
- To mimic the Model's original modeling stance, select Sample Bind-position from the Pose menu at the bottom of the Avatar window.
- To construct a bone-mapping from an initial posture, go to Mapping > Automap.
- Select Pose > Enforce T-Pose to return the Model to the desired T-pose.

If the automapping fails totally or partially, we may manually assign bones by dragging them from the Scene or Hierarchy views. If Unity feels a bone is appropriate, it will display green on the Avatar Mapping tab; otherwise, it will appear red.

Changing the Pose

The T-position is the default stance required by Unity animation and is the best pose to build in any 3D modeling software. If, on the other hand, you did not use the T-pose to build our character and the animation does not operate as planned, we may reset the animation by selecting Reset from the Pose drop-down menu:

If the bone assignment is accurate, but the character is not in the proper posture, the message "Character not in T-Pose" will appear. We can attempt to correct this by selecting Enforce T-Pose from the Pose option. If the position remains incorrect, manually rotate the other bones into a T-pose.

How to Make an Avatar Mask

Masking allows us to remove some of the animation data from a clip, enabling it to animate specific bits of an object or figure rather than the entire thing. For example, we may have a conventional walking animation that includes both arm and leg action, but if a character carries a massive object with both hands, we wouldn't want their arms swinging to the side while they walk. We could, however, utilize the usual walking animation while carrying the object by masking the upper body element of the carrying animation and playing it over the top of the walking motion.

Masking may be applied to animation clips during import or runtime. Masking during import time is desirable since it allows rejected animation data to be removed from our build, making the files smaller and therefore consuming less RAM. It also speeds up processing because less animation data need to be combined at runtime. Import masking may not be appropriate for your needs in some circumstances. In such a situation, we may apply a mask at runtime by generating an Avatar Mask Asset and utilizing it in our Animator Controller's layer settings.

To make an empty Avatar Mask Asset, you can do one of two things:

1. From the Assets menu, select Create > Avatar Mask.
2. In the Project view, choose the Model object for which we wish to define the mask, then right-click and select Create > Avatar Mask.

ADDING NON-HUMANOID (GENERIC) ANIMATIONS TO A MODEL

This section outlines how to import a model for use with Unity's Animation System. See Creating models for animation for information on how to create a model for use with the Animation System.

The Animation System supports two kinds of models:

1. A humanoid model is a specialized structure containing at least 15 bones that are structured to adhere to a real human skeleton loosely. Importing a model with humanoid animations includes instructions on how to do it.

2. Everything else is a Generic model. This might range from a teakettle to a dragon. This page offers information on how to import this type of model.

Outline

When we import a Generic model into Unity, we must specify which bone is the Root node. This effectively determines the center of mass of the model.

Generic setups do not use the Humanoid Avatar window since there is only one bone to map. Consequently, preparing to import a non-humanoid model file into Unity needs fewer steps than preparing a humanoid model.

- Configure our Rig to be Generic.
- By designing an Avatar Mask, you may limit the animation that is imported on certain bones.
- Enable the Import Animation option from the Animation menu, and then configure the other Asset-specific parameters.
- If the file has many animations or actions, we may use Animation Clips to define specified frame ranges.
- We may do the following for each Animation Clip described in the file:
  - Configure the posture and root transform.
  - Looping should be optimized.
  - To animate the timings of other things, add curves to the clip.

    - Add events to the clip to activate specific actions in sync with the animation.
    - Discard a portion of the animation the same way as a runtime Avatar Mask would, but this time at import time.
    - To drive the action, select a different Root Motion Node.
    - Read any messages from Unity regarding the import of the clip.
    - View a sneak peek of the animation clip.
- Click the Apply button at the bottom of the Import Settings box to preserve our changes, or Revert to undo them.

Setting Up the Rig

Set the Avatar (animation) type to Generic on the Inspector window's Rig tab. The Avatar Definition property is set to Create From This Model by default, and the Root node option is set to None.

In some circumstances, we may change the Avatar Definition option to Copy From Other Avatar to utilize an Avatar we already created for another Model file by changing the Avatar Definition option to Copy From Other Avatar. For example, suppose we construct a Mesh (skin) in your 3D modeling application with multiple individual animations. In that case, we may export the Mesh to a single FBX file and each animation to a separate FBX file.

When importing these files into Unity, we just need to make one Avatar for the first file (usually the Mesh). We may reuse that Avatar for the rest of the files as long as they all utilize the same bone structure.

If we keep the Create From This Model option selected, we'll need to choose a bone from the Root node property.

If we choose Copy From Other Avatar as the Avatar Definition option, we must indicate which Avatar you wish to use by selecting the Source attribute.

We can also modify the maximum number of bones impacting a specific vertex with the Skin Weights property. This parameter restricts impact to four bones by default, but we can select more or less.

Unity produces a Generic Avatar and adds an Avatar sub-Asset under the Model Asset in the Project view when clicking the Apply button.

It should be noted that the Generic Avatar is not the same as the Humanoid Avatar, although it does display in the Project view and has the Root node mapping. However, when we click on the Avatar icon in the Project view to expose its properties in the Inspector, only its name displays, and no Configure Avatar button appears.

How to Make an Avatar Mask

Masking may be applied to animation clips either during import or at runtime. Masking during import time is desirable since it allows rejected animation data to be removed from our build, making the files smaller and therefore consuming less RAM. It also speeds up processing because less animation data need to be combined at runtime.

Import masking may not be appropriate for our needs in some circumstances. In such a situation, we may apply a mask at runtime by generating an Avatar Mask Asset and utilizing it in our Animator Controller's layer settings.

To make an empty Avatar Mask Asset, we can do one of two things:

1. From the Assets menu, select Create > Avatar Mask.
2. In the Project view, choose the Model object for which we wish to define the mask, then right-click and select Create > Avatar Mask.

We may now select which bones to include or omit from a Transform hierarchy before adding the mask to an Animation Layer or adding a reference inside the Mask portion of the Animation tab.

Model Import Settings Dialogue Box

Bear in mind that these options are only for importing models and animations made in most 3D modeling software. Models built in SketchUp and SpeedTree, on the other hand, make use of particular parameters. See SketchUp Settings and SpeedTree Import Settings for further details.

When we place Model files in our Unity Project's Assets folder, Unity automatically imports and saves them as Unity Assets. Select the file in the Project window to open the Inspector window and examine the import settings. Set the settings on the four tabs on this window to modify how Unity imports the specified file:

A 3D Model might depict a person, a structure, or a piece of furniture. Unity generates numerous Assets from a single model file in certain circumstances. The main imported item in the Project window is a model Prefab. Typically, the model Prefab will additionally reference several Mesh objects.

A Rig (also known as a skeleton) is a collection of deformers organized in a hierarchy that animate a Mesh (also known as skin) on one or more models built in a 3D modeling application such as Autodesk® 3ds Max® or Autodesk® Maya®. Unity generates an Avatar for Humanoid and Generic (non-humanoid) Models to reconcile the imported Rig with the Unity GameObject.

As an Animation Clip, we may describe any number of various stances that occur throughout a set of frames, such as walking, running, or simply idling (moving from one foot to the other). We may reuse clips for any Model with the same Rig. A single file may include numerous distinct actions, each of which may be defined as a separate Animation Clip.

Materials and textures can be extracted or left included in the model. You may also change how Material is represented in the Model.

THE MODEL TAB

When we pick a Model, the Import Settings for that Model display on the Model tab of the Inspector window. These options have an impact on the Model's numerous components and attributes. Unity imports each Asset using these parameters; thus, we may change any settings to apply to various Assets in our Project.

This section contains information on each of the Model tab's sections:

A. Scene-level settings, such as whether to import Lights and Cameras and what scale factor to apply.

B. Meshes-specific properties.

C. Geometry-related features, such as topology, UVs, and normals.

Scene

Property	Function
Scale Factor	When the original file scale (from the Model file) does not meet the specified scale in your Project, set this value to apply a global scale to the imported Model, the physics system in Unity expects 1 meter in the game world to equal 1 unit in the imported file.
Convert Units	Enabling this option causes the Model scaling defined in the Model file to be converted to Unity's scale.
Bake Axis Conversion	When we import a Model that utilizes a different axis system than Unity, enable this feature to bake the results of axis conversion directly into our application's Asset data (for example, vertex or animation data). Disable this parameter to adjust the root GameObject's Transform component at runtime to mimic axis conversion.
Import BlendShapes	Allow Unity to import blend shapes with our Mesh by enabling this feature. For further information, see Importing blend shapes.
Import Visibility	Import the FBX parameters that determine whether MeshRenderer components are enabled or not (visible).

(Continued)

Property	Function
Import Cameras	Cameras from our .FBX files can be imported.
Import Lights	Lights from our .FBX file should be imported.
Preserve Hierarchy	Even if this model only has one root, always generate an explicit prefab root. As an optimization tactic, the FBX Importer usually removes any empty root nodes from the model. If we have multiple FBX files with different parts of the same hierarchy, we may use this option to keep the original structure. File1.fbx, for example, has a rig and a Mesh, but file2.fbx contains the same rig but simply the animation for that rig. If we import file2.fbx without checking this box, Unity removes the root node, the hierarchies do not match, and the animation breaks.
Sort Hierarchy By Name	Enable this feature to rank GameObjects inside the hierarchy alphabetically. To keep the hierarchical order defined in the FBX file, disable this parameter.

Blend Shapes Importing

Unity supports blend shapes (morphing) and can import blend shapes from 3D modeling programs' FBX and DAE files. Animated FBX files can also be imported. Blend forms on vertices, normals, and tangents may be animated at the vertex level in Unity.

Meshes can be affected by both skins and blend forms at the same time. When Unity imports Meshes with blend shapes, it utilizes the SkinnedMeshRenderer component (rather than the MeshRenderer component), yet if the mesh has skin or not.

Unity imports blend shape animation as part of standard animation: it animates blend shape weights on SkinnedMeshRenderers.

To import blend shapes using normals, use one of the two following methods:

1. Set the Blend Shape Normals to attribute to Import so that Unity may use the FBX file's normals.

2. Set the Blend Shape Normals option to Compute, and Unity will use the same logic to calculate normals on a Mesh and blend shapes.

Visibility Importing

The Import Visibility feature in Unity may read visibility properties from FBX files. By adjusting the Renderer.enabled property, values and animation curves can activate or disable MeshRenderer components.

Visibility inheritance is enabled by default, although it may be disabled. For example, if a parent Mesh's visibility is set to 0, all children's renderers are similarly disabled. In this scenario, one animation curve is constructed for each Renderer.enabled parameter of the child.

Some 3D modeling software does not support or have restrictions on visibility attributes. More information may be found at:

- Importing Models from Autodesk® Maya® into Unity has several limitations.

- Importing Blender models into Unity has certain limitations.

Cameras Importing

When importing Cameras from an .FBX file, Unity supports the following properties:

Property	Function
Projection mode	Perspective or orthographic. Animation is not supported.
Field of View	Animation is supported.
All Physical Camera characteristics	When we import a Camera with Physical Properties (for example, from Maya), Unity builds a Camera with the Physical Camera attribute enabled and the values from the FBX file for Focal Length, Sensor Type, Sensor Size, Lens Shift, and Gate Fit.
Near and Far Clipping Plane distance	On these settings, Unity does not import any animation. Enable the Clip Manually setting when exporting from 3ds Max; otherwise, the default settings are used on import.
Target Cameras	When importing a Target Camera, Unity constructs a camera with a LookAt constraint that uses the source as the target object.

Light Import

The following light kinds are supported:

- Spot.
- Omni.
- Area.
- Directional.

Light characteristics such as the ones listed below are supported:

Property	Function
Range	If UseFarAttenuation is enabled, the FarAttenuationEndValue is utilized. Animation is not supported by FarAttenuationEndValue.
Color	Animation is supported.
Intensity	Animation is supported.
Spot Angle	Animation is supported. Spot lights are the only ones that have this option.

Restrictions

Scaling on light characteristics is used in several 3D modeling applications. For example, we may change the light cone by scaling a spot light based on its hierarchy. Because Unity does not perform this, lighting may seem different in the game.

The width and height of area lights are not defined in the FBX format. Some 3D modeling software lacks this feature and must rely on scaling to determine the rectangular region. As a result, when imported, area lights always have a size of 1.

Targeted light animations aren't supported unless they're baked.

THE RIG TAB

The Rig tab options control how Unity assigns the deformers to the Mesh in the imported Model to be animated. This entails giving or establishing an Avatar for humanoid characters. This entails locating a Root bone in the skeleton for non-humanoid (Generic) characters.

When we pick a Model in the Project view, Unity automatically calculates which Animation Type best suits the Model and presents it in the Rig tab. If the file has never been imported into Unity, the Animation Type is set to None.

Property	Function
Animation Type	Specify the animation style.
None	There is no animation.
Legacy	The Legacy Animation System should be used. Import and utilize animations in the same way as we did in Unity 3.x and before.
Generic	If our rig is not humanoid, use the Generic Animation System (quadruped or any entity to be animated). Unity chooses a root node for us, but we may specify another bone to serve as the root node instead.
Humanoid	If our rig is humanoid, use the Humanoid Animation System (two legs, two arms, and a head). Unity typically recognizes the skeleton and accurately transfers it to the Avatar. In some circumstances, we may need to update the Avatar Definition and manually configure the mapping.

Types of Generic Animation

Avatars are not used in Generic Animations, as they are in Humanoid Animations. We must indicate which bone is the Root node since the skeleton might be arbitrary. The Root node enables Unity to maintain consistency across Animation clips for a Generic model and blend appropriately between Animations that were not created "in place" (that is, where the whole model moves its world position while animating).

Specifying the root node assists Unity in distinguishing between the movement of the bones relative to one another and the movement of the Root node in the environment (controlled from OnAnimatorMove).

Property	Function
Avatar Definition	Select where we want to acquire the Avatar definition.
Create from this model	Create an Avatar with this model.
Copy from Other Avatar	Point to an Avatar that has been set up on another model.
Root Node	Choose a bone to serve as the Avatar's root node. This option is only accessible if the Avatar Definition is set to Create From This Model.
Source	Import animation clips from another Avatar with the same setup. If the Avatar Definition is set to Copy from Other Avatar, this feature is only available.
Skin Weights	Set a maximum number of bones that can influence a single vertex.
Standard (4 Bones)	Use a maximum of four bones to exert maximum influence. This is the default option and is preferred for best results.
Custom	Set our limit for the number of bones. The Max Bones/Vertex and Max Bone Weight attributes appear when we pick this option.
Max Bones/ Vertex	Set the maximum number of bones that a specific vertex can influence. We can specify one to 32 bones per vertex; however the more bones we utilize to impact a vertex, the higher the performance penalty. This option is only accessible if the Skin Weights parameter is set to Custom.

(Continued)

Property	Function
Max Bone Weight	Set the lower limit for taking into account bone weights. The weighting formula disregards anything less than this number, and Unity ramps up bone weights more than this value to a total of 1.0. Only if the Skin Weights attribute is set to Custom is this option available.
Optimize Game Object	Remove and save the imported character's GameObject Transform hierarchy in the Avatar and Animator component. When enabled, the character's SkinnedMeshRenderers utilize the internal skeleton of the Unity animation system, which increases the performance of animated figures. If the Avatar Definition is set to Create From This Model, this option is only available.
Extra Transforms to Expose	When Optimize Game Object is enabled, we may specify which Transform routes Unity should disregard. See Including Extra Transforms for further details. This section is only shown if Optimize Game Object is enabled.

TAB AVATAR MAPPING

When the Unity Editor is in Avatar Configuration mode, the Avatar Mapping tab appears.

To enter Avatar Configuration mode, do one of the following:

1. In the Project window, choose the Avatar Asset and then click "Configure Avatar" in the Inspector, or
2. Select the Model Asset in the Project window, navigate to the Inspector's "Rig" tab, and click "Configure…" under the Avatar Definition menu.

When we are in Avatar Configuration mode, the Inspector displays the Avatar Mapping tab, which displays Unity's bone mapping:

A. Toggle between the Mapping and Muscles & Settings tabs using these buttons. Before going between tabs, we must Apply or Revert any changes we've made.

B. Buttons for switching between the Avatar's sections: Body, Head, Left Hand, and Right Hand.

C. Menus with numerous Mapping and Pose tools to assist us in mapping the bone structure to the Avatar.

D. Buttons for accepting modifications (Accept), reverting changes (Revert), and exiting the Avatar window (Done). Before exiting the Avatar window, we must Apply or Revert any changes we've made.

Avatar Data Saving and Reuse

The mapping of bones in our skeleton to the Avatar can be saved on disc as a Human Template file (extension *.ht). This mapping may be used for any character. For example, suppose we want to commit the Avatar mapping to source control and prefer text-based files; or suppose we want to parse the file with our custom tool.

Choose Store from the Mapping drop-down option at the bottom of the Avatar window to save the Avatar data in a Human Template file.

Unity shows a dialogue window in which we may specify the name and location of the saved file.

To load a previously prepared Human Template file, go to Mapping > Load and pick the file.

Making Use of Avatar Masks

It might be advantageous to limit animation to particular body parts at times. For example, in a strolling motion, the figure may sway their arms, but if they pick up a torch, they should hold it up to shed light. An Avatar Body Mask may be used to determine which areas of a character's animation should be confined to.

THE AVATAR MUSCLE AND SETTINGS TAB

Using Muscles, we may control the range of motion of various bones in Unity's animation system.

When the Avatar is appropriately set, the animation system "understands" the bone structure and allows us to use the Muscles & Settings tab of the Avatar's Inspector. Use the Muscles & Settings page to fine-tune the character's range of motion and verify that the character deforms convincingly, without visual artifacts or self-overlaps.

The Muscle & Settings tab has the following sections:

A. Switches between the Mapping and Muscles & Settings tabs. Before going between tabs, we must Apply or Revert any changes we've made.

B. Manipulate the character using predetermined deformations in the Muscle Group Preview box. These have an impact on many bones at the same time.

C. Adjust particular bones in the body using the Per-Muscle Settings section. We may adjust the range limitations of any option by expanding the muscle settings. For example, Unity's Head-Nod and Head-Tilt parameters have a default range of −40 to 40 degrees, but you may drop these ranges even more to stiffen these motions.

D. Adjust particular effects in the body using the Additional Settings.

E. The Muscles menu has a Reset button that resets all muscle parameters to their preset levels.

F. Buttons for accepting modifications (Accept), reverting changes (Revert), and exiting the Avatar window (Done). Before exiting the Avatar window, we must Apply or Revert any changes we've made.

Changes Being Previewed

We may see the changes in the Muscle Group Preview and Per-Muscle Settings sections right in the Scene view. We can view the range of mobility for each setting applied to our character by dragging the sliders left and right.

Through the Mesh, we can see the skeleton's bones.

Degree of Freedom Translate

To enable translation animations for the humanoid, activate the Translate DoF option in the Additional Settings. When this option is deactivated, Unity only uses rotations to animate the bones. Translation DoF is accessible for the following muscles: Chest, UpperChest, Neck, LeftUpperLeg, RightUpperLeg, LeftShoulder, and RightShoulder.

Enabling Translate DoF may raise performance requirements since the animation system must execute an additional step to retarget humanoid animation. As a result, we should only use this option if we know our animation incorporates animated translations of some of our character's bones.

THE WINDOW FOR AVATAR MASK

There are two methods for specifying which elements of our animation should be masked:

1. By choosing a humanoid body map.
2. By specifying which bones should be included or excluded from a Transform hierarchy.

Choosing a Humanoid Body

If our animation includes a Humanoid Avatar, we may use the simplified humanoid body diagram to determine where to hide the animation.

The body diagram divides the body into the following sections:

- Head.
- Right Arm.
- Left Arm.
- Right Hand.
- Left Hand.
- Right Leg.
- Left Leg.
- Root.

To add motion to one of these bodily parts, click the Avatar diagram for that part until it turns green. To turn off animation, click the body part until it turns red. Double-click the empty space around the Avatar to include or omit everything.

Toggle Inverse Kinematics__ (IK)__ for hands and feet, which regulates whether or not IK curves are included in animation mixing.

Selection of a Transform

If our animation does not employ a Humanoid Avatar, or if we want more control over which specific bones are masked, we can pick or deselect elements of the Model's hierarchy:

- Assign a reference to the Avatar whose transformation we want to hide.
- Select the Import Skeleton option. In the inspector, we can see the avatar's hierarchy.
- We may check each bone in the hierarchy to see which one we want to use as our mask.

Mask Assets can be utilized in Animator Controllers when defining Animation Layers or in the import settings of our animation files to apply masking during the import animation.

Masks have the advantage of reducing memory overheads since body parts that are not active do not require their corresponding animation curves. Furthermore, the unused curves do not need to be computed during playback, which reduces the animation's CPU cost.

HUMAN TEMPLATE WINDOW

A Human Template file (*.ht) is a YAML file that holds a humanoid bone mapping for a Model that we saved in the Avatar window.

The contents of Human Template files are shown as ordinary Unity text fields in the Human Template window.

Each grouping corresponds to a YAML file entry, with the name of the bone mapping target labeled First and the name of the bone in the Model file labeled Second.

This attribute allows us to alter most of the data in this file; however, any modification we make to the file is instantaneously updated by Unity. We may, however, undo any changes made while this window is open.

ANIMATION WINDOW INSTRUCTIONS

The Animation Window in Unity allows us to create and edit Animation Clips from within the program. It is intended to be a strong and simple alternative to external 3D animation applications. In addition to animating movement, the editor allows us to animate material and component variables and supplement our Animation Clips with Animation Events, which are functions that are invoked at specific times along the timeline.

MAKING USE OF THE ANIMATION VIEW

In Unity, the Animation view is used to examine and modify Animation Clips for animated GameObjects. In Unity, navigate to Window > Animation to get the Animation view.

Viewing Animations on a GameObject

The Hierarchy window, the Project window, the Scene view, and the Inspector window are all related to the Animation window. The Animation window, like the Inspector, displays the timeline and keyframes of the Animation for the currently chosen GameObject or Animation Clip Asset. We may select a GameObject from the Hierarchy window or the Scene View, or we can select an Animation Clip Asset from the Project Window.

The List of Animated Properties

The Animation view (left) displays the Animation used by the currently chosen GameObject and any child GameObjects controlled by this Animation. The Scene and Hierarchy views are on the right, indicating that the Animation view displays the Animations associated with the currently chosen GameObject.

A list of animated attributes may be seen on the left side of the Animation view. This list is empty in a newly produced clip when no animation has yet been captured.

When we start animating specific attributes in this clip, the animated properties will display here.

If the animation controls many child objects, the list will also include hierarchical sub-lists of the animated attributes of each child item. Different sections of the Robot Arm's GameObject hierarchy are animated within the same animation clip in the preceding example.

When animating a hierarchy of GameObjects within a single clip, ensure the Animation is created on the root GameObject in the hierarchy.

Each property may be folded and unfolded to display the precise values captured at each keyframe. The value fields display the interpolated value if the playback head (the white line) is between keyframes. We may directly modify these fields.

When adjustments are made while the playback head is over a keyframe, the values of that keyframe are updated if modifications are made when the playback head is between keyframes, a new keyframe with the new value that we input is produced at that point.

A property in the Animation View has been unfurled, enabling the keyframe value to be put in directly.

Timeline of Animation

The timeline for the current clip is shown on the right side of the Animation View. This timeline displays the keyframes for each animation property. The timeline view is available in two modes: Dopesheet and Curves. Go to the bottom of the animated property list area and click Dopesheet or Curve to switch between these modes.

These provide two different perspectives on the Animation timeline and keyframe data.

Timeline Mode in Dopesheet

Dopesheet mode provides a more condensed view, letting us see each property's keyframe sequence on its horizontal track. This provides a quick summary of the keyframe timing for several properties or GameObjects.

Timeline Mode for Curves

Curves mode shows a resizable graph that shows how the values of each animation attribute vary over time. Within the same graph view, all chosen attributes display the stack.

This mode gives us complete control over how the values are shown and edited and how they are interpolated between them.

Fitting Our Choice to the Window

When viewing our Animation in Curves mode, remember that the varied ranges for each parameter might vary substantially at times. Consider an introductory Animation clip of a spinning, bouncing cube. The bouncing Y position value may range from 0 to 2 (meaning the cube bounces two units high during the animation); however, the rotation value can range from 0 to 360. (representing its degrees of rotation). When viewing these two curves concurrently, the animation curves for the position values will be difficult to discern since the view will be zoomed out to suit the 0–360 range of rotation values inside the window.

The position and rotation curves of a bouncing spinning cube are chosen, but because the screen is zoomed out to meet the rotation curve's 0–360 range, the bouncing Y position curve is difficult to distinguish.

To zoom in on the currently selected keyframes, press F on the keyboard. This is excellent for quickly focusing and resizing the window on a section of our Animation timeline for better editing.

Click on specific properties in the list and hit F on the keyboard to re-scale the display to suit the value range. We may also manually magnify the Curves window by dragging the handles at either end of the view's scrollbar sliders. The Animation Window is zoomed in to show the bouncing Y position Animation. The beginning of the yellow rotating curve is still visible, but it has now extended well beyond the top.

To fit and re-scale the window to show all the keyframes in the clip, press A on the keyboard. If we wish to see the entire timeline while keeping your current selection, try this.

Controls for Playback and Frame Navigation

Use the Playback Controls at the upper left of the Animation view to control the playback of the Animation Clip.

These are the controls, from left to right:

- Toggle preview mode on/off.
- Recording mode (on/off) If record mode is enabled, the preview mode is always enabled.
- Set the playback head to the start of the clip.
- Reposition the playback head to the previous keyframe.
- The animation should be played.
- Navigate the playback head to the next keyframe.
- Place the playback head at the conclusion of the clip.

We may also control the playback head using the keyboard shortcuts listed below:

- To return to the previous frame, press the Comma (,).
- To go to the next frame, use the Period (.) key.
- To return to the previous keyframe, hold Alt and hit Comma (,).
- To go to the next keyframe, hold Alt and hit Period (.).

Window Locking

We may prevent the Animation editor window from automatically switching to reflect the currently chosen GameObject in the Hierarchy or Scene by locking it. Locking the window is essential if we want to concentrate on the Animation of one GameObject while still selecting and manipulating other GameObjects in the Scene.

MAKE A NEW ANIMATION CLIP

Select a GameObject in our Scene and open the Animation Window to create a new Animation Clip (top menu:) Animation may be accessed via Window > Animation > Animation.

If no Animation Clips have been added to the GameObject, the "Create" button shows in the Animation Window timeline area.

Select the Create option. Unity invites us to save our newly created empty Animation Clip to our Assets folder.

Unity does the following actions when you save this new empty Animation Clip:

- This function generates a new Animator Controller Asset.
- The new clip is added as the default state to the Animator Controller.
- Adds an Animator Component to the GameObject to which animation is being applied.
- The new Animator Controller is assigned to the Animator Component.

Including Another Animation Clip

The "Create" button is not shown if the GameObject already has allocated one or more Animation Clips. In the Animation window, instead, one of the existing clips is displayed. To switch between Animation Clips, utilize the menu located in the top-left corner of the Animation window, next to the playback controls.

Select Create New Clip from this menu to add a new Animation Clip to an existing GameObject's animations. Before we can start on your new empty Animation Clip, Unity invites us to save it.

How It All Works Together

The preceding steps automatically create the necessary components and references. It is, nonetheless, beneficial to understand how the components fit together.

- An Animator component is required for a GameObject.
- An Animator Controller Asset must be attached to the Animator component.
- One or more Animation Clips must be attached to the Animator Controller Asset.

Following the creation of a new Animation Clip, we will now be able to see:

- The Animation Window (top left) displays a timeline with a white playback headline, ready for recording new keyframes. The name of the clip may be seen in the clip menu, directly below the playback controls.

- The Inspector (center) reveals that the "Cube" GameObject contains an Animator Component. The Controller field of the component reveals that it is assigned to an Animator Controller Asset named Cube.
- The Project Window (bottom right) displays two new Assets: an Animator Controller Asset called Cube and an Animation Clip Asset called Cube Animation Clip.
- The Animator Window (bottom left) displays the Animator Controller's contents. There is a Cube Animation Clip on the controller, and it is in the default state (as indicated by the orange color). Subsequent clips added to the controller are grey, indicating that they are not in the default condition.

ADDING ANIMATION TO A GAMEOBJECT

After we've saved the new Animation Clip Asset, we can start adding keyframes to the clip.

In the Animation window, we have two options for animating GameObjects: Record Mode and Preview Mode.

1. **Record Mode:** When we move, rotate, or otherwise adjust any animatable property on our animated GameObject in record mode, Unity automatically produces keyframes at the playback head. To enable record mode, press the button with the red circle. When in record mode, the Animation window time line is shaded red.
2. **Preview Mode:** Modifying our animated GameObject in preview mode does not immediately produce keyframes. Each time we change the state of your

GameObject, we must manually add keyframes (for example, moving or rotating it). To enable preview mode, click the Preview button. When in preview mode, the Animation window time line is shaded blue.

Keyframes Recording

Click the Animation Record button to start recording keyframes for the selected GameObject. This activates Animation Record Mode, which records changes to the GameObject into the Animation Clip.

Once in Record mode, we may add keyframes by dragging the white Playback head to the desired time on the Animation time line and then modifying our GameObject to the correct state at that point in time.

Changes to the GameObject are saved as keyframes at present, shown by the white line in the Animation Window.

Any modification to an animatable property (such as its position or rotation) will result in the appearance of a keyframe for that property in the Animation window.

Selecting or dragging in the time line bar changes the playback head and displays the status of the animation at the current time of the playback head.

The Animation window is seen in record mode. The time line bar has a red tint, indicating that it is in record mode, and the animation properties have a red backdrop in the inspector.

By pressing the Record button again, we can exit the Record Mode at any moment. When we exit Record mode, the Animation window transitions to Preview mode, allowing us to see the GameObject at its current position along the animation time line.

We may animate any GameObject property by altering it while in Animation Record Mode. Moving, rotating, or scaling the GameObject adds keyframes to the animation clip for those attributes.

While in Record mode, adjusting values directly in the GameObject's inspector inserts keyframes. This is true for each animatable property in the inspector, including numeric values, checkboxes, colors, and the majority of other values.

Any GameObject attributes that are now animated are listed on the left side of the Animation Window. This window does not display properties that are not animated. Any new properties that you animate, including those on child objects, are added to the property list area as soon as they are active.

Transform attributes are unique in that the .x, .y, and .z properties are connected, allowing curves to be inserted for all three simultaneously.

By pressing the Add Property button, you may also add animatable properties to the current GameObject (and its descendants). When we click this button, a list of the GameObject's animateable characteristics appears in a pop-up window.

These correspond to the properties specified in the inspector.

The white vertical line in Preview or Record mode indicates which frame of the Animation Clip is presently being previewed. The GameObject is visible in the Inspector and Scene View at that frame of the Animation Clip. The animated properties' values at that frame are also displayed in a column to the right of the property names.

Time Line

We may shift the playback head to any frame on the Animation window time line by clicking anywhere and then previewing or adjusting that frame in the Animation Clip. The numbers on the time line are shown in seconds and frames; thus, 1:30 equals one second and thirty frames.

In Preview Mode, You May Create Keyframes

In addition to using Record mode to produce keyframes automatically when you alter a GameObject, we may create keyframes in Preview mode by modifying a GameObject property and then manually choosing to create a keyframe for that property.

In preview mode, animation properties in the Inspector window are shaded blue. When we notice this blue tint, it implies that these values are being driven by the animation clip's keyframes that are now displayed in the animation window.

If we change any of these blue-tinted properties while previewing, the GameObject enters a changed animation state. This is indicated by a pink hue shift in the tone of the inspection field. Because we are not in record mode, your change has not yet been stored as a keyframe.

Making Keyframes by Manually

When we have edited a GameObject in preview mode, there are three ways to generate a keyframe manually.

We may add a keyframe by right-clicking the property label of the property we've updated and selected

"Add a keyframe for just that property" or "Add a keyframe for all animated properties":

When we add a keyframe, the new keyframe appears as a diamond symbol in the animator window. The property field returns to a blue tint, indicating that our change was stored as a keyframe and that we are now seeing a value driven by the animation keyframes.

In the Animation window, we can also create a keyframe by clicking the Add Keyframe button:

Alternatively, we may insert a keyframe using the hotkeys K or Shift-K, as indicated below:

- **Keyboard shortcuts:**
    - **K:** Key all animated. Adds a keyframe for all animated properties in the animation window at the current location of the playback head.
    - **Shift-K:** Modify all keys. Only adds a keyframe for animated properties that have been changed at the current location of the playback head in the animation window.

CONTROLLERS FOR ANIMATORS

An Animator Controller is used to create and manage a collection of animations for a character or other animated Game Object.

The controller contains references to the animation clips utilized inside it. It controls the many animation states and transitions among them using a State Machine, which may be thought of as a flowchart or a basic program written in Unity's visual programming language.

UNITY'S NAVIGATION SYSTEM

We may design characters that can travel the game environment using the Navigation System. It enables our characters to comprehend that they must use stairs to reach the second storey or leap to cross a ditch. The Unity NavMesh system is made up of the following components:

- NavMesh (short for Navigation Mesh) is a data structure that defines the game world's walkable surfaces and allows us to identify a path from one walkable area to another. The data structure is generated automatically based on your level geometry.
- The NavMesh Agent component allows us to design characters who avoid one other as they go toward their goal. Agents use the NavMesh to reason about the gaming world, and they know how to avoid each other as well as moving obstacles.
- The Off-Mesh Link component enables us to provide navigation shortcuts that a walkable surface cannot represent. Off-mesh linkages include things like jumping over a ditch or a fence or unlocking a door before stepping through it.
- We may use the NavMesh Obstacle component to define moving impediments that agents avoid while navigating the globe. An obstacle is anything like a barrel or a container that is regulated by the physics system. The agents try their best to avoid the obstacle while it is moving. Still, once it gets stationary,

it will cut a hole in the NavMesh so that the agents may modify their courses to steer around it, or if the stationary obstruction is blocking the primary way, the agents can choose another route.

Designing User Interfaces (UI)

Unity offers three UI systems for creating UI for the Unity Editor and apps created in the Unity Editor:

1. The Unity UI package.
2. UI Toolkit.
3. IMGUI.

Toolkit for UIs

The UI Toolkit is Unity's newest UI system. It is built on standard web technologies and is intended to improve performance across platforms. When we install the UI Toolkit package, we may use it to develop extensions for the Unity Editor as well as runtime UI for games and applications.

The UI Toolkit comprises the following:

- A retained-mode UI system including the essential features and capabilities necessary to construct UIs is included in the UI Toolkit.
- Types of UI Assets are influenced by standard web formats such as HTML, XML, and CSS. Use them to organize and style UIs.
- Tools and resources for learning how to use UI Toolkit, as well as developing and debugging interfaces.

Unity wants UI Toolkit to be the default UI system for new UI development projects, although it lacks several functionalities present in Unity UI (uGUI) and IMGUI.

The Unity UI Package

The Unity UI (Unity UI) package (also known as uGUI) is an older, GameObject-based UI framework for developing runtime UI for games and apps. You utilize components and the Game view to structure, position, and design the UI in Unity UI. It has powerful text and rendering functions.

Immediate Mode Graphical UI

Immediate Mode Graphical UI is a code driven UI Toolkit that draws and manages UIs using the OnGUI function and scripts that implement it. IMGUI may be used to construct custom Inspectors for script components, Unity Editor extensions, and in-game debugging displays. It is not recommended for creating runtime UIs.

Choosing a UI System for our Project

Unity wants UI Toolkit to be the default UI system for new UI development projects, although it lacks several functionalities present in Unity UI (uGUI) and IMGUI. These older technologies are superior in specific use situations and must be supported in order to sustain legacy projects.

The type of UI system you select for a specific project is determined by the type of UI you intend to create and the features we require support.

Audio

Full 3D spatial sound, real-time mixing and mastering, mixer hierarchies, snapshots, preconfigured effects, and many more capabilities are available in Unity Audio. This includes in-game sounds as well.

That said, we will turn our attention to Performance Optimization in the next chapter.

CHAPTER 5

Scene Performance Optimization

Now that we have created and handled Scenes, it is time to turn our attention toward actual performance optimization.

APPLICATION PROGRAMMING INTERFACE (API) SUPPORT FOR GRAPHICS

Unity supports the DirectX, Metal, OpenGL, and Vulkan graphics APIs, depending on the API's availability on a given platform. Unity employs either a pre-installed set of graphics APIs or the graphics APIs that you specify in the Editor.

To utilize Unity's default graphics APIs, follow these steps:

- Navigate to the Player settings (Edit > Project Settings, then pick the Player category).
- Navigate to Other Settings and tick the Auto Graphics API box.

DOI: 10.1201/9781003214755-5

When the Auto Graphics API for a platform checkbox is selected, the Player build contains a set of built-in graphics APIs and utilizes the best one at runtime to deliver the best case scenario.

When the Auto Graphics API for a platform is unchecked, the Editor employs the first API in the list. To observe how our program performs on OpenGL in the Editor, for example, drag OpenGLCore to the top of the list, and the Editor switches to OpenGL rendering.

Uncheck the applicable Auto Graphics API, click the addition (+) button, then select the graphics API from the drop-down box to override the default graphics APIs for the Editor and Player.

The default API is the graphics API at the top of the Auto Graphics API list. If the platform does not support the default API, Unity falls back to the following API in the Auto Graphics API list.

See Platform-specific rendering differences for information on how graphics rendering differs between systems and Shader language semantics. Only a fraction of graphics APIs allows tessellation and geometry shaders. The Shader Compilation Target level governs this.

DirectX

Navigate to the Player settings (menu: Edit > Project Settings, then choose the Player category) and select DirectX11 as our chosen Graphics API in the Editor or Standalone Player. Disable the Auto Graphics API for Windows setting and select DirectX11 from the drop-down menu.

Shaders for the Surface

Because some sections of the Surface Shader compilation pipeline do not comprehend DX11-specific HLSL syntax, we must wrap it in a DX11-only preprocessor macro if we use HLSL features like StructuredBuffers, RWTextures, and other non-DX9 vocabularies.

Geometry Shaders and Tessellation

Surface Shaders support simple tessellation and displacement.

We may use the entire range of DX11 Shader model 5.0 capabilities when manually building Shader programs, including Geometry, Hull, and Domain Shaders.

Only a fraction of graphics APIs allows tessellation and geometry shaders. The Shader Compilation Target level governs this.

Shaders Computed

Compute Shaders are graphics card-based programs that can speed up rendering.

Metal

Metal is Apple's industry-standard graphics API. Unity works with Metal on iOS, tvOS, and macOS (Standalone and Editor).

On Apple systems, Metal provides more features than OpenGL ES.

Metal has the following advantages:

- Reduce the CPU overhead associated with graphics API requests.
- The API validation layer.
- On multi-graphics processing unit (GPU) systems, better GPU control.

- On iOS/tvOS, memory-less render targets are supported.
- Apple has established a new norm.
- Shaders for computers.
- Shaders for tessellation.

The drawbacks of using Metal:

- There is no support for low-end devices.
- Geometry shaders are not supported.

Restrictions and Requirements

- The Metal support is available in iOS and tvOS for Apple A7 or newer SoCs.
- The Metal support is available in macOS for Intel HD and Iris Graphics from the HD 4000 series or later, AMD GCN-based GPUs, and Nvidia Kepler-based GPUs or later.
- The minimum shader compilation goal is 3.5.
- Metal does not support geometry shaders.

Metal Enabling

To set Metal the default graphics API for the Unity Editor and Standalone Player, perform one of the following:

- Go to the Edit > Project Settings menu in the Editor, choose the Player category, and activate Metal Editor Support.

- Alternatively, if we're using macOS, launch Terminal and use the -force-metal command line parameter.

- On iOS, tvOS, and macOS Standalone Players, Metal is enabled by default.

Metal API Validation

Metal API validation is provided by Xcode and may be used to track down obscure bugs. To enable Metal API validation in Xcode, follow these steps:

- Create an iOS project in Unity. This produces an Xcode project.

- In Xcode, open the produced Xcode project and choose Edit Scheme.

Core OpenGL

OpenGL Core is a backend that can handle the most recent OpenGL capabilities on Windows, macOS X, and Linux. Depending on the OpenGL driver support, this ranges from OpenGL 3.2 to OpenGL 4.5.

Activating OpenGL Core

Navigate to the Player settings (menu: Edit > Project Settings, then choose the Player category) and navigate to Other Settings to designate OpenGL Core as your preferred Graphics API in the Editor or Standalone Player. Disable the Auto Graphics API for Windows property and select OpenGLCore from the drop-down menu.

OpenGL Specifications

The following are the minimal requirements for OpenGL Core:

- Mac OS X 10.8 (OpenGL 3.2), Mac OS X 10.9. (OpenGL 3.2 to 4.1).
- Windows has used NVIDIA GPUs since 2006 (GeForce 8), AMD GPUs since 2006 (Radeon HD 2000), and Intel GPUs since 2012 (HD 4000/IvyBridge) (OpenGL 3.2 to OpenGL 4.5).
- GNU/Linux (OpenGL 3.2 to OpenGL 4.5).

Limitations of the macOS OpenGL Driver

OpenGL 3.x and 4.x capabilities such as tessellation and geometry shaders are supported by the macOS OpenGL backend for the Editor and Standalone.

However, Apple limits the OpenGL version on the Mac OS X desktop to 4.1 at maximum. It does not support all DirectX 11 capabilities (such as Unordered Access Views or Compute Shaders). This implies that any shaders set to target Shader Level 5.0 (by #pragma target 50) will fail to load on OS X.

As a result, a new shader target level is added: #pragma target gl4.1. This target level necessitates at least OpenGL 4.1 or DirectX 11.0 Shader Level 5 on a desktop or OpenGL ES 3.1 + Android Extension Pack on a mobile device.

Features of OpenGL Core

The new OpenGL back-end adds a slew of new functionality (formerly limited to DX11/GLES3):

- Shaders that compute (together with ComputeBuffers and "random write" render textures).
- Shaders for tessellation and geometry.
- Indirect drawing (Graphics.DrawProcedural. Graphics.DrawProceduralIndirect).
- Modes of the advanced blend.

Command-Line Parameters for the OpenGL Core Profile

The following command-line options can be used to launch the editor or player using OpenGL:

- **-force-opengl:** Forces the usage of the legacy OpenGL backend.
- **-force-glcore:** Forces the usage of the latest OpenGL back-end. With this parameter, Unity will identify all of the features that the platform supports to run with the best OpenGL version and all accessible OpenGL extensions.
- **-force-glcoreXY:** The value of XY can be 32, 33, 40, 41, 42, 43, 44, or 45, with each number signifying a different version of OpenGL. If the platform does not support a given version of OpenGL, Unity will fall back to a supported version.
- **-force-clamped:** Request that Unity does not employ OpenGL extensions, ensuring that the same code path is executed on different systems. This is a method for determining whether a problem is platform-specific (a driver bug, for example).

Native OpenGL ES Command-Line Parameters on Desktop

The OpenGL ES graphics API is accessible on Windows computers with Intel or NVIDIA GPUs with OpenGL ES drivers.

- **-force-gles:** Forces the new OpenGL backend to be used in OpenGL ES mode. With this parameter, Unity will identify all of the features that the platform supports to run with the best OpenGL ES version and all accessible OpenGL ES extensions.
- **-force-glesXY:** The value of XY can be 20, 30, 31, 31aep, or 3.2, with each number signifying a different version of OpenGL ES. If the platform does not support a given version of OpenGL ES, Unity will fall back to a supported version. Unity will utilize an alternative graphics API if the platform does not help OpenGL ES.
- **-force-clamped:** Request that Unity does not employ OpenGL extensions, ensuring that the same code path is executed on different systems. This is a method for determining whether a problem is platform-specific (a driver bug, for example).

GRAPHICS PERFORMANCE OPTIMIZING

Many games rely on a strong performance to be successful. Here are some essential tips for increasing the speed of our game's rendering.

Find High-Impact Graphics

The graphical elements of our game might have a significant influence on two computer systems: the GPU and the CPU. Because tactics for optimizing for GPU vs. CPU are generally different (and might even be contrary—for example, it's fairly usual to make the GPU do more work when optimizing for CPU, and vice versa), the first rule of any optimization is to discover where the performance problem is.

Common bottlenecks and how to detect them:

- GPU performance is frequently constrained by fill-rate or memory bandwidth.
    - Reduce the display resolution and start the game. If lowering the display resolution makes the game run quicker, you may be limited by GPU fillrate.
- The CPU is frequently constrained by the number of batches that must be rendered.
    - In the Rendering Statistics panel, choose "batches." The greater the number of batches rendered, the greater the cost to the CPU.

Less common bottlenecks include:

- There are too many vertices to process on the GPU. The number of vertices suitable for excellent performance is determined by the GPU and the complexity of vertex shaders. In general, strive for no more than 100,000 vertices on mobile. Even though a PC can handle several million vertices, it is still best to keep this number as low as possible through optimization.

- There are too many vertices for the CPU to handle. Skinned meshes, fabric simulation, particles, and other game elements and meshes might all benefit from this. As previously stated, it is typically best practice to keep this number as low as possible without sacrificing game quality.
- If rendering is not an issue on the GPU or CPU, there may be a fault somewhere, such as in our script or physics. To pinpoint the issue, use the Unity Profiler.

CPU Enhancement

To render things on the screen, the CPU must conduct considerable processing work, such as detecting whether lights effect that object, establishing the shader and shader parameters, issuing drawing orders to the graphics driver, and preparing the commands for graphics card transmission.

All of this "per object" CPU utilization is resource-intensive, and it may pile up if you have a lot of visible items. For example, if we have a thousand triangles, it is much easier on the CPU, and they're all in one mesh rather than one mesh per triangle. The cost of both cases on the GPU is roughly comparable, but the CPU effort required to render a thousand items is much greater.

Reduce the number of visible objects. To minimize the amount of work the CPU must perform:

- Combine nearby items manually or with the help of Unity's draw call batching.
- By combining individual textures into a more prominent texture atlas, you may use fewer materials in your models.

- Reduce the number of items that cause objects to be displayed several times (such as reflections, shadows, and per-pixel lights).

Combine items such that each mesh has at least a few hundred triangles, and just one Material is used for the whole mesh. It's worth noting that joining two things that don't share a substance yields any performance boost. The most common cause for requiring multiple materials is that two models do not share the same textures, ensure that any objects you combine have the same textures to improve CPU efficiency.

Combining objects may not make sense when utilizing many pixel lights in the Forward rendering process.

OnDemandRendering CPU Optimization

OnDemandRendering can help you enhance CPU performance by allowing you to change the rendering pace of your application.

In the following cases, we may want to reduce the frame rate:

- **Menus, such as the application's launcher or a pause menu:** Menus are often primary sequences that do not require full-speed rendering. To save power and limit the device temperature from rising to the point where the CPU frequency is throttled, we can draw menus at a lower frame rate.

- **Chess and other turn-based games:** Players either wait for other users to move or think about their move. During moments of low activity, we can reduce the frame rate to avoid wasting power and extending battery life.

- Applications with largely static material, such as Automotive user interface (UI).

Adjusting the rendering speed allows you to regulate power consumption and device thermals to maximize battery life and avoid CPU throttling. It's especially effective when used with the Adaptive Performance package. Even when frames are displayed less often, the program continues to deliver events to scripts at a standard rate (for example, it may accept input during a non-rendered frame). We may use OnDemandRendering to avoid input latency. renderFrameInterval = 1 for the input length to keep motions, buttons, and so on responsive.

This API is not helpful for situations that require a lot of programming, physics, animation, but not rendering. Visuals in our program may stall with no impact on power utilization.

VR apps do not support demand rendering. When not rendering every frame, the graphics go out of sync with head movement, potentially increasing the risk of motion sickness.

GPU: Model Geometry Optimization

There are two primary rules for maximizing a Model's geometry:

1. Use no more triangles than are necessary.
2. Reduce the amount of ultraviolet (UV) mapping seams and harsh edges.

It is crucial to note that the actual number of vertices that graphics hardware must process is not always the same as the number presented by a three-dimensional (3D) application. Modeling software often displays the number of different corner points that comprise a model (known as the geometric vertex count). However, some geometric vertices must be divided into two or more logical vertices for rendering reasons on a graphics card.

If a vertex has several normals, UV coordinates, or vertex colors, it must be divided. As a result, the vertex count in Unity is generally more than the count provided by the 3D application.

While the quantity of geometry in Models is most significant for the GPU, several Unity also features process Models on the CPU (for example, Mesh skinning).

Lighting Efficiency

The quickest method is to produce lighting that does not require any computation at all. To do this, utilize Lightmapping to "bake" static lighting once rather than compute it per frame. The process of creating a lightmapped environment in Unity takes only a bit longer than simply adding a light in the area, but:

- It is significantly quicker (two–three times faster for two per-pixel lighting).
- It looks much better now that you can bake global illumination and use the lightmapper to smooth the results.

In many circumstances, simple approaches may be used instead of installing several more lights. Instead of adding a light that shines directly into the camera to create a Rim Lighting effect, include a specialized Rim Lighting calculation right into our shaders (see Surface Shader Examples to learn how to do this).

Forward Drawing of Lights

Per-pixel dynamic lighting increases the amount of rendering effort required for each impacted pixel, resulting in objects being drawn in numerous passes. On less powerful devices, such as mobile or low-end PC GPUs, avoid having more than one Pixel Light illuminating any one item and instead utilize lightmaps to light static objects rather than calculating their lighting every frame. Because per-vertex dynamic lighting may add a large amount of effort to vertex transformations, avoid instances where numerous lights illuminate a single object.

Combining models that are far enough to be influenced by various sets of pixel lighting is not a good idea. Each mesh must be rendered as many times as the number of pixel lights that illuminates it when using pixel lighting. When two meshes that are very far apart are joined, the effective size of the resultant object grows. Because all pixel lights that illuminate any area of this composite object are considered during rendering, the number of rendering passes required might be increased. In general, the number of passes required to render the combined item equals the total of the number of passes needed to draw each component object; hence, merging meshes yields no benefit.

During rendering, Unity detects all lights in the vicinity of a mesh and determines which of those lights most influence it. The Quality window parameters control how many lights are pixel lights and how many are vertex lights. Each light calculates its value depending on how distant it is from the mesh and how bright its illumination is—and certain lights are more essential than others merely based on the game scenario. As a result, each light has a Render Mode setting that can be set to either Important or Not Important; lights identified as Not Important have a smaller rendering overhead.

Consider a driving game where the player's automobile is driving in the dark with the headlights turned on. Because the headlights are the most visually noticeable light source in the game, their Render Mode should be set to Important. Other lights in the game, such as other cars' backlights or distant lampposts, may be less relevant and may not increase the visual impression much by becoming pixel lights. To prevent wasting rendering power in regions where it is ineffective, set the Render Mode for such lights to Not Important.

Per-pixel lighting optimization saves both CPU and GPU work: the CPU has fewer draw calls, and the GPU has fewer vertices to compute and pixels to rasterize for all the additional object renderings.

Texture Compression and Mipmaps on the GPU

Compressed textures can be used to reduce the size of your textures. This can lead to faster load times, a reduced memory footprint, and much-improved rendering speed. Uncompressed 32-bit RGBA textures need a fraction of the memory bandwidth required by compressed textures.

Mipmaps for Textures

Always turn on Make mipmaps for textures in a 3D environment. For tiny triangles, a mipmap texture allows the GPU to use a lower resolution texture. This is analogous to how to texture compression can help limit the amount of texture data transmitted by the GPU when rendering.

The only exception is when a texel (texture pixel) is known to map 1:1 to a visible screen pixel, like in UI components or a two-dimensional (2D) game.

LOD and Cull Distances Per Layer

Culling items entails making them invisible. This is an efficient method for reducing both CPU and GPU burdens.

In many games, culling small items more aggressively than large ones is a quick and effective technique without sacrificing the user experience. Small pebbles and rubbish, for example, may be made invisible from a great distance while massive buildings remain visible.

There are various techniques we might use to do this:

- Make use of the Level Of Detail mechanism.
- Set the camera's per-layer culling distances manually.
- Put little items on a separate layer and use the Camera.layerCullDistances script function to build up per-layer cull distances.

Shadows in Real Time

Realtime shadows are lovely, but they may significantly impact speed, both in terms of more CPU draw calls and extra GPU processing.

GPU: Guidelines for Creating High-Performance Shaders

Performance capabilities vary significantly between platforms; a high-end PC GPU can handle far more graphics and shaders than a low-end mobile GPU. A fast GPU is dozens of times quicker than a poorly integrated GPU, even on the same platform.

GPU efficiency on mobile platforms and low-end PCs will almost certainly be significantly lower than on your development computer. To obtain decent performance across low-end GPU devices, it's advised that we manually tune your shaders to decrease calculations and texture reads. Some built-in Unity shaders, for example, have "mobile" versions that are substantially quicker but have some limits or approximations.

Complex Mathematical Operations Transcendental mathematical functions (such as pow, exp, log, cos, sin, tan) consume many resources, thus using them sparingly. If applicable, consider employing lookup textures as an alternative to complex math operations.

Avoid developing our businesses (such as normalize, dot, inversesqrt). The built-in features in Unity ensure that the driver generates significantly better code. Keep in mind that the Alpha Test (discard) action frequently slows down our fragment shader.

The Precision of Floating Points While floating-point variables' precision (float vs. half vs. fixed) is often overlooked on desktop GPUs, it is critical for mobile GPU performance.

A Simple Checklist to Help Us Improve Our Game's Speed

- When creating for PC, keep the vertex count around 200K and the frame count under 3M. (depending on the target GPU).
- Choose shaders from the Mobile or Unlit category if we're utilizing built-in shaders. They are also compatible with non-mobile systems; however, they are reduced and approximated counterparts of the more complicated shaders.
- Keep the number of distinct materials per scene as little as possible, and share as many materials as feasible across various items.
- To enable internal optimizations such as static batching, set the Static attribute on a non-moving object.
- Instead of multiples, use a single (ideally directed) pixel light to affect our geometry.
- Rather than utilizing dynamic lighting, bake lighting.
- When feasible, choose compressed texture formats and 16-bit textures over 32-bit textures.
- When at all possible, avoid employing fog.
- In complicated static scenes with many occlusions, use Occlusion Culling to limit the amount of visible geometry and draw-calls. Consider occlusion culling while creating our levels.
- Skyboxes can be used to "fake" distant geometry.

- Instead of a multi-pass technique, use pixel shaders or texture combiners to combine several textures.
- When feasible, use half-precision variables.
- Reduce the usage of complex mathematical operations in pixel shaders such as pow, sin, and cos.
- Reduce the number of textures per fragment.

Batching of Draw Calls

The engine must submit a draw call to the graphics API in order to draw a GameObject on the screen (such as OpenGL or Direct3D). Draw calls are frequently resource-intensive, with the graphics API performing substantial work for each draw request, resulting in CPU performance overhead. This is primarily due to state changes made between draw calls (such as switching to a new Material), which need resource-intensive validation and translation processes in the graphics driver.

To remedy this, Unity employs two methods:

1. **Dynamic batching:** for small enough Meshes, this changes the vertices on the CPU, combines several similar vertices together, and draws them all at once.
2. **Static batching:** aggregates static (non-moving) GameObjects into large Meshes, which are then rendered more quickly.

As opposed to manually merging GameObjects together, built-in batching has various advantages; the most important is that GameObjects may still be culled separately.

However, it has certain drawbacks; static batching incurs memory and storage expense, whereas dynamic batching incurs some CPU overhead.

Material Preparation for Batching

Only GameObjects with the same Material can be batched. As a result, if you want to achieve effective batching, try to distribute Materials across as many distinct GameObjects as feasible.

If you have two similar Materials that only differ in texture, you may merge their Textures into a single large Texture. A texture atlas is a term used to describe this procedure. Once Textures are in the same atlas, a single Material can be used instead.

Only GameObjects with the same Material can be batched. As a result, if we want to achieve effective batching, try to distribute Materials across as many distinct GameObjects as feasible.

If we have two similar Materials that only differ in texture, we may merge their Textures into a single large Texture. A texture atlas is a term used to describe this procedure. Once Textures are in the same atlas, a single Material can be used instead.

If we need to access shared Material properties from scripts, keep in mind that changing Renderer.material produces a duplicate of the Material. To keep Materials shared, use Renderer.sharedMaterial instead.

Even though their Materials are different, shadow casters can typically be batched together during rendering. In Unity, shadow casters can employ dynamic batching with various Materials as long as the values in the Materials required by the shadow pass are the same. Many crates, for example, might employ Materials with different Textures on them, but the textures are irrelevant for shadow caster drawing; therefore, they can be batched together in this scenario.

Dynamic Batching

If two GameObjects have the same Material and meet additional requirements, Unity can automatically batch move them into the same draw call. Dynamic batching occurs automatically and requires no further effort on our part.

- Because batching dynamic GameObjects incurs some expense per vertex, it is limited to Meshes with no more than 900 vertex attributes and no more than 300 vertices.
  - We may batch up to 300 verts if our Shader uses Vertex Position, Normal, and single UV, but only 180 verts if our Shader uses Vertex Position, Normal, UV0, UV1, and Tangent.
- GameObjects cannot be batched if the transform contains mirroring (for example, GameObject A with +1 scale and GameObject B with –1 scale cannot be batched together).
- Using separate Material instances prevents GameObjects from batching together, even if they are otherwise identical. The shadow caster rendering is an exception.
- Lightmap-enabled GameObjects have two new renderer parameters: lightmap index and offset/scale

into the lightmap. In general, dynamic lightmapped GameObjects should all point to the exact lightmap location to be batched.

- Multi-pass shaders break batching.
    - Almost all Unity Shaders allow multiple Lights in forwarding rendering, essentially performing additional passes for them. The "extra per-pixel lights" requested in the draw are not batched.
    - Because it must draw GameObjects twice, the Legacy Deferred (light pre-pass) rendering approach disables dynamic batching.

Because dynamic batching works by translating all GameObject vertices into world space on the CPU, it is only helpful if the effort is less than that of a draw call. The resource needs of a draw call are determined by various factors, the most important of which is the graphics API utilized. For example, on consoles or contemporary APIs like Apple Metal, the draw call cost is often substantially more minor, and dynamic batching is often ineffective.

Dynamic Batching (Particle Systems, Line Renderers, Trail Renderers)

Dynamic batching works differently for components with geometry generated dynamically by Unity than it does for Meshes.

- Unity merges all batchable material for each suitable renderer type into a single big Vertex Buffer.
- The renderer creates the batch's Material state.

- The Vertex Buffer is bound to the Graphics Device by Unity.
- Unity changes the offset in the Vertex Buffer for each Renderer in the batch before submitting a new draw request.

When calculating the cost of Graphics Device calls, the setup of the Material state is the slowest component of drawing a Component. In comparison, submitting draw calls at multiple offsets into a standard Vertex Buffer is extremely fast.

This method is quite similar to how Unity submits draw calls when Static batching is used.

Batching That Is Static

Static batching enables the engine to decrease draw calls for the geometry of any size as long as it is made of the same material and does not move. It is frequently more efficient than dynamic batching (since it does not convert vertices on the CPU), but it consumes more memory.

To use static batching, we must explicitly define that particular GameObjects are static and do not move, rotate, or scale in the game. To do so, use the Inspector's Static checkbox to mark GameObjects as static.

Static batching necessitates the use of extra memory to store the combined geometry. If numerous GameObjects shared the same geometry before static batching, a duplicate of that geometry is made for each GameObject, either in the Editor or at runtime. This isn't always a smart idea; to preserve a lower memory footprint, we may have to trade rendering performance by eliminating static batching for some GameObjects. For example, labeling trees as static at a thick forest level might have a significant memory influence.

Static batching works internally by converting static GameObjects into world space and creating a single shared vertex and index buffer for them. If we activate Optimized Mesh__ Data__ (in the Player settings), Unity eliminates vertex elements that are not utilized by any shader variation while constructing the vertex buffer. To do this, certain specific keyword checks are used; for example, if Unity does not detect the LIGHTMAP ON keyword, it eliminates lightmap UVs from a batch. Then, for visible GameObjects in the same batch, Unity executes a series of basic draw calls with essentially no state changes in between.

Technically, Unity does not preserve API draw calls but rather the state changes between them (which is the resource-intensive part). On most systems, batch limitations are 64k vertices and 64k indices (48k indices on OpenGLES, 32k indices on macOS).

Instancing of GPUs

Using a limited number of draw calls, use GPU Instancing to draw (or render) several copies of the same Mesh simultaneously. This is handy for sketching items that recur regularly in a Scene, such as houses, trees, grass, or other things.

Each draw call merely produces identical Meshes, but each instance might have various parameters (for example, color or size) to add diversity and lessen the perception of repetition.

GPU Instancing has the potential to minimize the number of draw calls utilized per Scene. This dramatically increases our project's rendering performance.

Including Instancing in Our Materials

To enable GPU Instancing on Materials, choose our Material in the Project window and click the Enable Instancing option in the Inspector.

This checkbox appears in Unity only if the Material Shader supports GPU Instancing. This covers all surface Shaders as well as Standard, StandardSpecular, and StandardSpecular.

GPU Instancing is enabled, while it is not in the bottom image. Take note of the differences in FPS, Batches, and Time Saved by Batching.

The following constraints apply when using GPU instancing:

- Unity automatically selects MeshRenderer and Graphics components. Instancing is required by DrawMesh. It should be noted that Skinned MeshRenderer is not supported.

- In a single GPU instancing draw call, Unity only groups GameObjects with the same Mesh and Material. To improve instancing efficiency, use a limited amount of Meshes and Materials. Modify our shader scripts to include per-instance data to generate variations.

Displaying the Statistics Window

The Game view includes a statistics box that displays real-time rendering information about your program during Play mode. Select the Stats button in the upper right corner to open this window. The window appears as an overlay in the upper right corner of the Game view. Its statistics are essential for optimizing performance. The specific statistics accessible depend on the build target.

Statistics

Statistics	Description
FPS	Updates to the frame per second, Unity performs.
CPU	The overall amount of time required to process one frame. This includes the time Unity took to execute our application's frame update and the time Unity spent in the Editor updating the Scene view, other Editor Windows, or other Editor-only operations. Rendering time: The number of times it takes to render one frame. This figure includes the time Unity took to render the Game View, but not the time Unity used in the Editor to render the Scene View or create the Inspector.
Batches	The total number of batches processed by Unity during a frame. This figure contains both static and dynamic batches, as well as, for instance, batches.
Saved by batching	The total number of batches created by Unity. Share materials across distinct GameObjects as often as feasible to guarantee optimal batching. Changing the rendering state divides batches into groups that have the same state.
Tris	The amount of triangles processed by Unity during a frame. This is especially true when optimizing for low-end hardware.
Verts	The number of vertices processed by Unity during a frame. This is especially true when optimizing for low-end hardware.
Screen	The screen's resolution, as well as the quantity of RAM it employs.

(Continued)

Statistics	Description
SetPass	The number of times Unity changes between shader passes while rendering GameObjects during a frame. A shader can have several shader passes, each of which renders GameObjects in the scene differently. Each pass necessitates the binding of a new shader, which may result in CPU cost.
Shadow casters	The number of GameObjects in the frame that throw shadows.
Visible skinned meshes	Unity rendered the amount of Skinned Mesh Renderers in the frame.
Animations	The amount of animations that are active throughout the frame.

Debugger for Frames

The Frame Debugger allows us to stop a running game on a specific frame and inspect the individual draw calls used to create that frame. In addition to identifying the draw calls, the debugger allows us to walk through them one at a time, allowing us to examine in great detail how the Scene is built from its graphical pieces.

Making Use of Frame Debugger

Frame Debugger window (menu: Window > Analysis > Frame Debugger) displays draw call information and allows us to change the "playback" of the frame as it is being created.

The main list displays the series of draw calls (and other events such as framebuffer clean) in a hierarchy that specifies where they originated. More information about the draw call is shown in the panel to the right of the list, including geometry data and the shader used for rendering.

When we choose an item from the list, the Scene, including the draw call, is presented entirely. The left and right arrow buttons on the toolbar and the arrow keys go forward and backward in the list in a single step. Furthermore, the slider at the top of the window allows us to swiftly "scrub" through the draw calls to find an item of interest. When a draw call corresponds to the geometry of a GameObject, the item is highlighted in the main Hierarchy window to aid identification.

If the selected draw call renders into a RenderTexture, the contents of that RenderTexture are displayed in the Game view. This is handy for studying how different off-screen render targets, such as the diffuse G-buffer in deferred shading, are constructed:

The debugger of Remote Frames

To use Frame Debugger remotely, the player must support multithreaded rendering (for example, WebGL does not support it; thus, frame debugger cannot operate on it), most Unity platforms enable it, and you must pick the "Development Build" option while creating.

Note for Desktop platforms: check the "Run In Background" option before building; otherwise, when we connect Frame Debugger to the player, it won't reflect any rendering changes until it has focus; assuming you're running both Editor and the player on the same machine, when you control Frame Debugger in Editor, we'll take the focus away from the player.

Quickly Begin:

- Build the project from the Editor to the target platform (select Development Player).
- The player should be run.

- Return to the Editor.
- Launch the Frame Debugger window.
- Active Profile Rendering, animating, or in our game logic.
- When you click Enable, the frame debugger should be enabled on the player.

Options for Render Target Display

A toolbar at the top of the information panel allows us to isolate the red, green, blue, and alpha channels for the current state of the Game view. Similarly, using the Levels slider to the right of these channel buttons, we may separate sections of the display based on brightness levels. These options are only available when rendering into a RenderTexture.

When rendering into several render targets simultaneously, we may choose which one to show in the game view. The diffuse, specular, normals, and emission/indirect lighting buffers are shown in 5.0 deferred shading mode.

We may also view the depth buffer contents by selecting "Depth" from the dropdown menu.

By isolating the render texture's alpha channel, we can observe the occlusion (stored in RT0 alpha) and smoothness (stored in RT1 alpha) of the delayed G-buffer.

This Scene's emission and ambient/indirect lighting are rather dark; we may make them more apparent by using the Levels slider.

Streaming of Mip Maps

We may control which mipmap levels Unity loads into memory using the Mip Map Streaming mechanism. Unity must draw the current Camera position in a Scene rather than loading them by default since it just loads the mipmaps; this technique reduces the overall amount of memory Unity requires for Textures. It sacrifices a small amount of CPU resources for the possibility of saving a substantial quantity of GPU memory.

We may also establish a total memory limit for all Textures in a Project using the Memory Budget. To keep under this limit, the Mip Map Streaming mechanism automatically cuts mip map levels.

The Mip Map Streaming API may be used to request particular mip map levels for specified Textures. Unity includes example C# code that replicates the engine logic for mip map selection, which we may use to alter the engine logic in our Projects.

Mip Map Streaming saves 25–30% of Texture RAM in Unity's Viking Village sample project, depending on Camera placement.

To Begin With

To enable Mip Map Streaming, navigate the Quality Settings in Unity (Edit > Project Settings > Quality) and tick the Texture Streaming checkbox. This displays the Mip Map Streaming system's options.

Then, for each Texture, activate Mip Map Streaming to allowing the Mip Map Streaming system to stream each Texture's mip maps from the disc into memory. To do so, choose the Texture to which we wish to apply Mip Map Streaming, then go to the Inspector window and look at the Texture Import settings. Enable the Streaming Mip Maps option in the Advanced settings.

If we're working on Android, you also need to enter the Build Settings and change the Compression Method to LZ4 or LZ4HC. For asynchronous Texture loading, Unity requires one of these compression algorithms, on which the Mip Map Streaming system is based.

Unity loads mip maps with the best feasible resolution while adhering to the Texture Memory Budget. Use the C# API to provide mip map levels for each Texture for more precise control or fine-tune the Mip Map Streaming system's automated output.

Restrictions

Mipmap Streaming can be told to compute the required mipmap levels using one of the ways listed below:

- Each Texture is allocated to a Material, which is subsequently assigned to a Unity Renderer.
- Texture2D.requestedMipmapLevel is used to request mip levels manually.

Unity cannot determine which mip level to utilize if we do not instruct Mipmap Streaming to generate mipmap levels using one of these ways. As a result, Unity loads the texture with low-quality mips that seem fuzzy.

The systems listed below do not use conventional Renderers. This implies that we must manually configure the desired mipmaps for these systems; otherwise, Unity will utilize low-resolution textures:

- Textures for decal projectors.
  - **Reflection meter Textures:** Lower resolution mipmaps serve as a roughness lookup table. As a

result, if Unity chooses a lower mipmap level, it renders materials with incorrect roughness.

    - **Textures in the Terrain system of Unity:** Mipmap Streaming on Terrain Textures is not supported by Unity. This is because Terrain Textures must be available at full quality at all times for Unity to tile and mix the textures.

- Shaders that behave differently than Unity's built-in shaders when it comes to texture UV coordinates. Unity always expects that textures are sampled using UV0 and saved in the Msh. Any shader-based changes to the texture coordinates, with the exception of scale and translation, or the use of UV1, are ignored.

When a renderer is running, the mesh the renderer is using requires accurate UV distribution metrics to determine the required mipmap level. As part of the mesh importing procedure, Unity automatically generates dispersion metrics. This may also be calculated in a script using Mesh.GetUVDistributionMetric.

When Unity displays a streaming Texture via an API (such as Graphics.DrawMeshNow), the system lacks the renderer limits and other information needed to determine the mip level; therefore, we must manually define the Texture mip level (or disable Mipmap Streaming on this Texture).

Mipmap Streaming Troubleshooting

Unity has a Mipmap Streaming debugging view mode. To access it, pick Texture Streaming from the Scene view control drop-down menu. Depending on their state in the Mipmap Streaming system, this view mode tints GameObjects the following colors:

- Green for textures with decreased mipmaps as a result of the Mipmap Streaming technology.
- Textures with fewer mipmaps are shown in red because the Mipmap Streaming system does not have the resources to load them.
- Textures that are not configured to stream, or if there is no renderer calculating the mip levels, are shown in blue.

Using the Debugging API, we can also create our own debug tools and visualizations.

CHAPTER 6

Completing the Game

As of now, we have covered all the basics pertaining to Unity, right from installation and setup to scene management, optimization, and world physics.

However, at times our code might run into certain problems. This is where debugging comes in to play.

DEBUGGING C# CODE IN UNITY

We may view our source code while our application or game is running by using a debugger. The following code editors are available for debugging C# programs in Unity:

- Visual Studio (in conjunction with the Visual Studio Tools for Unity plug-in).
- Visual Studio for Mac is a software development tool.

DOI: 10.1201/9781003214755-6

- Rider by Jetbrains.
- Code in Visual Studio.

Although the debugger capabilities supported by these code editors differ widely, they all enable essential functions such as break points, single stepping, and variable examination.

Except for WebGL, managed code debugging in Unity works on all platforms. It is compatible with the Mono and IL2CPP scripting backends.

Setting up the Code Editor

- **In Visual Studio (Windows):** The installer for the Unity Editor gives the option to install Visual Studio together with the Visual Studio Tools for Unity plug-in. This is the recommended method for configuring Visual Studio for debugging with Unity.

  If we already have Visual Studio installed on our computer, navigate the Tools > Get Tools and Features… menu to find and install the Visual Studio Tools for Unity plug-in.

- **In Visual Studio for Mac:** The installation for Unity Editor gives the option to install Visual Studio for Mac. This is the recommended method for installing Visual Studio for Mac in order to debug with Unity.

  If we already have Visual Studio for Mac installed on our computer, utilize its Extension Manager to find and install the Visual Studio Tools for Unity plug-in.

- **JetBrains Rider:** The JetBrains Rider installation by default can debug code in Unity on Windows or Mac. To install it, please go to the JetBrains website.

- **VS Code:** To debug code in Unity, we must install the relevant extension from VS Code. For instance, the Debugger for Unity: https://marketplace.visualstudio.com/items?itemName=Unity.unity-debug or the Unity Tools extension: https://marketplace.visualstudio.com/items?itemName=Tobiah.unity-tools.

Choosing an External Script Editor in Unity

After installing a code editor, navigate to Preferences > External Tools and change the External Script Editor to our preferred code editor.

Editor Debugging

We can debug the C# code that is running in the Unity Editor while it is in Play Mode.

To debug in the Editor, change the Editor's Code Optimization mode to Debug Mode, then attach a code editor with debugging capabilities.

To change the Code Optimization mode, click the Debug button in the Unity Editor Status Bar's bottom right corner.

The Code Optimization Option in Unity Offers Two Options

1. Debug Mode, which allows us to attach external debugger software, results in reduced C# performance when running our Project in the Editor in Play Mode.

2. When we run our Project in Play Mode in the Editor, we get quicker C# performance, but we can't attach any external debuggers.

When we click the Debug button in the status bar, a little pop-up window appears with a mode switch button. It also shows information about the current mode and explains what occurs when we switch modes.

To modify the mode in which the Unity Editor launches, navigate to Edit > Preferences > General > Code Optimization On Startup.

Use the following API to control these settings from a script: Compilation.Compilation, ManagedDebugger Compilation. CodeOptimization, and Pipeline-codeOptimization.

We can also alter the Editor's startup mode or disable the debugger listen to the socket. To accomplish this, run the Editor with the following command line arguments:

- **-releaseCodeOptimization:** Enables release code optimization in the Editor.
- **-debugCodeOptimization:** Enables debug code optimization in the Editor.
- **-disableManagedDebugger:** starts the Editor without the debuggers listening to the socket.

Attaching to the Editor and Setting Breakpoints

Set a breakpoint in our external code editor on a line of script code where the debugger should halt. For instance, in Visual Studio, click on the column to the left of our code on the line where we want to stop the debugger. A red line appears, highlighting the line.

```
Public class ExampleScript : MonoBehaviour
{
Use for initialization
```

```
Void Start()
{
Debug.Log("Debug message");
}
}
```

Next, connect the code editor to the Unity Editor. This option varies based on the code editor and is frequently distinct from the code editor's standard debugging procedure.

Some code editors may allow us to choose a Unity instance to debug. In Visual Studio, for example, the Debug > Attach Unity Debugger option offers this possibility.

Return to the Unity Editor and select Play Mode after the code editor has been attached. When the code at the breakpoint is run, the debugger will come to a halt, as shown below:

```
Public class ExampleScript : MonoBehaviour
{
Use for initialization
Void Start()
{
Debug.Log("Debug message");
}
}
```

We may inspect the contents of variables when the code editor is at a breakpoint. The Unity Editor will be inactive until we select the debugger's continue option or exit debugging mode.

In-Player Debugging

To analyze script code running in a Unity Player, first select the "Development Build" and "Script Debugging" options before constructing the Player (these choices may be found in File > Build Settings). Enabling the "Wait For Managed Debugger" option causes the Player to wait for a debugger to be attached before running any script code.

Select the IP address and port of our Unity Player to attach the code editor. The drop-down menu in Visual Studio's "Attach To Unity" option.

Android and iOS Device Debugging

- **Android:** When debugging a Player on an Android device, connect to it through USB or TCP. To connect to an Android device, for example, in Visual Studio (Windows), select Debug > Attach Unity Debugger.
- **Chrome OS with Android:** Unity is unable to detect Chrome OS devices automatically. To initiate a connection, connect to the device using its IP address using Android Debug Bridge (adb), and then manually enter the IP address in the debugging window.
- **Ios:** Connect to the device using TCP while debugging a Player running on an iOS device. To connect to an iOS device, for instance, in Visual Studio (Mac), select Debug > Attach Unity Debugger.

Using the Debugger to Troubleshoot

The majority of debugger issues occur because the code editor cannot identify the Unity Editor or Player. This signifies that it is unable to attach the debugger correctly. The network frequently generates connection problems since the debugger requires a TCP connection to the Editor or Player.

Here are some measures we may take to troubleshoot common connectivity problems.

Make Certain That the Debugger Is Attached to the Right Unity Instance

We may connect the code editor to any Unity Editor or Unity Player on our local network that supports debugging. When attaching the debugger, make sure we're attaching it to the right instance. If we know the device's IP address or machine name where we are executing the Unity Player, we may use it to find the relevant instance.

Check Our Network Connection to the Unity Instance

The code editors use the same logic as the Unity Profiler to find a Unity instance to debug. If the code editor cannot locate the Unity instance you need it to locate, try attaching the Unity Profiler to that instance. If the Unity Profiler can't discover it, there might be a firewall on the system where we're running the code editor or the machine where we're running the Unity instance (or possibly both).

Ascertain That the Device Only Has One Active Network Interface

A large number of gadgets have several network interfaces. A mobile phone, for example, may have both an active cellular connection and an active Wi-Fi connection. To successfully connect the debugger for TCP, the IDE must establish a network connection to the device's appropriate interface. If we intend to debug through Wi-Fi, for example, put the device in airplane mode to deactivate all other interfaces before enabling Wi-Fi.

In the Player Log, we can see the Unity Player's IP address instructing the IDE to use.

Examine the Firewall Settings

A TCP connection connects the Unity instance to the code editor. This TCP connection takes place on an arbitrary port on most Unity systems. Usually, we shouldn't need to know this port because the code editor will detect it for us. If it doesn't work, try using a network analysis tool to establish which ports could be restricted, either on the system where the code editor is running or on the machine or device where the Unity instance is running. When we've found the ports, make sure our firewall permits access to both the port on the code editor system and the port on the Unity instance machine.

Test to See if the Managed Debugging Information Is Available

If the debugger attaches, but no breakpoints are loaded, the debugger may not locate the code's controlled debugging information. Managed code debugging information is kept on disc in .pdb files alongside the managed assembly (.dll file).

When the appropriate settings and build parameters are enabled. Unity will automatically generate this debugging information. On the other hand, Unity cannot create this debugging information for controlled plugins in the Project. Debugging code from managed plugins is feasible if the associated.pdb files are in the Unity project on disc next to the managed plugins.

Prevent the Device from Locking

If the device we're using to debug the app has a screen lock, make sure it's turned off. Screen locks detach the debugger and prevent it from reconnecting. When debugging controlled programs, it is best to avoid locking the screen. If the screen does lock, we must restart the program on the device before reconnecting to the debugger.

TESTING OF UNITS

As our project develops in size and the number of scripts, classes, and methods grow, it can be challenging to verify that a change in one section of our code does not break things in another.

Automated testing allows us to ensure that all elements of our code are working correctly. It saves time by identifying where and when problems arise as soon as they are introduced during development instead of depending on manual testing or, worse, bug reports from our end users.

The Unity Test Framework package is a tool that allows us to test our code in both Edit and Play modes and on target platforms, including Standalone, Android, and iOS.

Appraisal

Unity is an all-purpose gaming engine that is popular for game creation across all paradigm. It supports both two-dimensional (2D) and two-dimensional (3D) graphics, as well as scripting in C# and drag-and-drop capability. It is a cross-platform gaming engine created by Unity Technologies. People used it to create simulations and video games for consoles, PCs, and mobile devices in their early days.

The first formal unveiling of Unity occurred in 2005 at Apple's Worldwide Developers Conference. It was only compatible with OS X at the time. It has now developed and expanded to target as many as 27 platforms. Despite its broad range of uses, Unity gets the most popular for its mobile game creation.

Hence, a large portion of their attention is directed toward mobile platforms as well.

WHAT DOES UNITY HAVE IN STORE FOR DEVELOPERS?

Unity is a powerful game engine that offers its creators a plethora of built-in functional capabilities. 3D rendering, physics, and collision detection are examples of these.

DOI: 10.1201/9781003214755-7

From the standpoint of a developer, this effectively eliminates the need to reinvent the wheel. It spares them from developing a new physics engine and defining all component materials' intrinsic properties and attributes from the start. The inclusion of a built-in Visual Studio and its C# scripting application programming interface (API) also works in its favor.

The availability of a thriving "Asset Store" is what endears Unity to its creators. The Asset Store allows developers to upload their works and share them with the rest of the community.

WHAT EXACTLY IS THE UNITY IDE?

Unity is also known as an Integrated Development Environment (IDE), apart from being just a game engine. This implies that Unity gives developers an interface via which they can access all necessary tools in one location.

Additionally, the Unity program has a visual editor that allows developers to alter the attributes of various objects and construct their scenes using the drag and drop tool.

Aside from that, Unity provides its users with a slew of additional helpful tools and capabilities. These include using a timeline tool to create animations and browse between several directories in a project. Unity provides you the option of switching to a different editor of your choosing to meet our coding needs.

WHAT IS THE LANGUAGE USED BY UNITY?

The Unity game engine employs C# in conjunction with several other related classes and APIs to deal with code and logic.

The most excellent thing about utilizing Unity is that it allows us to complete various jobs without requiring us to manage or understand a large amount of code. However, if we are proficient in coding, we will do far more on the platform than the ordinary user. Given how adaptable Unity is in tweaks and alterations, having a solid grasp of coding will undoubtedly offer us an advantage.

C# is a programming language that is exceptionally user-friendly for beginners. This is the fundamental reason why Unity has become the game production platform of choice, especially for young and inexperienced creators.

WHAT IS INCLUDED IN THE UNITY INTERFACE?

It is divided into the five sections listed below:

1. **Scene View:** This is the portion in which the developer designs the many levels for their 3D projects, games, and other sceneries. This category contains all of our design components and game items. We are free to modify them to meet your needs.
2. **Game View:** This is the area where we can see our outcomes. In essence, the Game View provides a good depiction of the scenario or level that we have in mind. However, to view this effect, a camera must be present on the scene. As a result, this part is also referred to as the Camera View Section.
3. **Hierarchy:** In the Hierarchy section, we will see all the game objects we have put directly in our scene or level. In a nutshell, we must register everything that the Game View displays. This applies to both visible and non-visual game items.

4. **Project:** The Project Window's job is to display the contents of the Assets folder on our disc. This part provides access to various aspects, including Scripts, Folders, Textures, Audio, Models, Video, and Game Objects.

5. **Inspector:** The Inspector panel allows us to view the many qualities and properties of each selected Game Object. The user's selection determines the components and characteristics that are presented.

NEW UNITY USERS SHOULD FOLLOW THIS ADVICE

Make Something

Most of the advice we've received for aspiring Unity developers, students, or newbies focuses on one basic guideline that extends beyond this specific engine: make something, even if it's just a straightforward game. Completing even a little endeavor from conception to completion has excellent worth.

"If we're just starting in game creation, we should simply do things and make them work in any way we can," Williams advises. "Then, if we accomplish that, we should subsequently broaden your horizons and attempt to understand topics outside of game creation, to go beyond and discover what more we can achieve than the standard Unity manner."

However, Playtonic's Price feels that without a framework, we should not enter.

"Set ourselves some targets and benchmarking tests and give it a shot," he suggests. "Don't base our decision just on our views and conjectures."

Discover How to Make Our Tools

After completing a few simple tasks, we should progress beyond the fundamentals and investigate other functionalities.

"Learn how to create our tools with Unity," Foster suggests. "It's all written in C#. Find out what our code does when it generates garbage. The garbage collector is a monster that will slow down our game when we attempt to place stuff on mobile, Switch, Xbox, and PS4. And if we build garbage-free code, our code will dash, and we won't have to worry about it again."

Make an Effort to Reach Out to the Community

If we're thinking about using Unity as our game engine, the good news is that its community is large enough that most of our problems are likely simply a Google search away from a solution. There are dozens of tutorials available for whatever degree of development, from novice to heavy optimizations, so we should lean on that community.

Gerges describes games as "interesting monsters," and he hasn't "worked on one yet that didn't produce proper head-scratching moments." And we're talking about someone who has been working in the games industry for 15 years. He continues: "We've benefited from the community and direct support from Unity on multiple occasions to help us overcome obstacles and challenging circumstances."

Price ends by highlighting. Unity's established track record creates amazing games across a wide range of platforms and genres that are already available.

"As a developer, regardless of the engine we choose, we must be innovative in how you utilize it to realize a goal," he adds. "Unity can construct whatever game our imagination can dream up."

IS THERE A HIGH NEED FOR UNITY DEVELOPERS?

Aside from the gaming business, an increasing number of sectors and companies perceive potential in employing Unity. The possibility of what this engine can achieve gives an incredible opportunity for Unity developers, who may anticipate multiple career prospects in the road.

As a Unity developer, we must keep an eye out for new features that Unity publishes and stay up to date to appeal to our future employer. Brush up on skills required in areas such as medical or automotive if we want to work in these professions.

The top Unity developers continuously learn and stay up to date on emerging game standards and development technology.

UNITY DEVELOPER—REQUIRED SKILLS

Unity web development necessitates specific abilities and expertise in video games.

A Unity developer will sometimes focus solely on the game's design and more creative aspects, while other times will focus exclusively on the code. An excellent idea would be to find a happy medium.

To construct sophisticated projects, absolute coding abilities (C#, UnityScript, Boo) are required. Unity developers must stay up to date on the current coding techniques in the game industry.

Furthermore, having a great visual sense is advantageous being able to create gorgeous interactive visuals is a crucial ability to have as a Unity Developer. If we want to improve our abilities, Unity's Asset Store has a wealth of materials that may assist game creators with minimal coding expertise. Visual scripting, for example, is available with PlayMaker or Bolt.

As Unity Developer, We Must Have the Following Skills

- Excellent understanding of Unity, including scripting, texturing, animation, GUI styles, and user session management.
- Scripts require C# programming expertise.
- Experience with level design and planning.
- Understanding of game physics and particle systems.
- Experience developing mobile and console games.
- Ability to minimize memory and space utilization for outdated hardware support.
- Extensive knowledge in 3D and 2D development.
- Experiment with Virtual Reality or Augmented Reality.
- Exceptional understanding of Object-Oriented Programming (OOP) and Data-Oriented Programming (DOOP).
- Extensive knowledge of the Entity Component System (ECS).

- Knowledge of contemporary design and architectural patterns.
- A talent for developing code that is clear, legible, and easy to maintain.
- Extensive experience with automated testing tools and unit tests.
- Understanding of code versioning tools (Git).

A UNITY DEVELOPER'S RESPONSIBILITIES

A Unity developer in the gaming business is creating games for numerous target platforms using the Unity framework.

Their key responsibility will be to translate design ideas, concepts, and requirements into a practical and exciting game. Dedication to collaborative problem solving, intelligent design, and a high-quality result is required.

What Responsibilities Does a Unity Developer Have?

- Implement game features following the stated design.
- Convert the design requirements into a playable game.
- Implement features in a quick and agile manner.
- Communicate with other team members to create an efficient pipeline and incorporate media assets.
- Create, design, and maintain code that is efficient, reusable, and dependable.

- Ensure that apps have the most excellent possible performance, quality, and responsiveness.
- Identify bottlenecks and glitches and come up with strategies to solve and minimize these issues.
- Integrate player input to improve game aspects.
- Assist in maintaining code quality, structure, and automation.
- Adding code to remote repositories like Git.

Index

A

B

E

F

G

H

I

N

O

P

Q

R

S

V

W

Y

Printed in the United States
by Baker & Taylor Publisher Services